WILDLIFE TALES & RURAL RIDES

MARC HARRIS

First published in Great Britain in 2018 by Marc Harris Publishing

Copyright © Marc Harris 2018

All rights reserved. No part of this publication may be reproduced, stored in a retrieval system or transmitted in any form, or by any means, electronic, mechanical, photocopying, recording or otherwise, without the prior written permission of the publisher.

A Cataloguing in Publication record for this book is available from the British Library

Printed by Orphans Press, Leominster

ISBN: 978-1-5272-2313-4

Cover photograph is of Howden Reservoir, the Peak District.

CONTENTS

TRAVEL WRITING

Cornish Time 9
In Search of Emperors 21
The Hidden Gems of Barry Island 24
In Memory of Mary Gillham, MBE 27
The Peregrine Diaries 30
The Beauty of Bute Park 33
Walking the Welsh Jurassic Coast 35
Sea Lamprey 37
Shellfish Curry 39
Cricket Balls and Kebabs 42

SHORT STORIES

A Seasoned Old Moth 47
No Ordinary Joe 49
Pit Ponies 51
She Stoops to Conquer 53
Lady of the Lake 55
The Mistress of the Wreck 57
The Specimen Hunter 60
A Tale of Two Riverbanks 62
The Boilie 65
The Undead 67
The Boy and the Brook 69
A Breed Apart 71
The Garden's Secrets 73

POEMS

Peregrines on the Clock Tower
    The Tiercel 77
    The Falcon 78
Sea Lamprey 79
Shoaling 80
The Ghosts of Greenfarm Hostel 81
Owl Night 82
Conger 83
The River Beckons for a Last Cast 84
The Wye 85
Spate 86
The River's Midden 87
The Fish Market 88
River Dreams 89
View from a River Bridge 90
A River Senses a Jogger at Night 91

INTRODUCTION

The title of this book, Wild Tales and Rural Rides – an anthology of short stories, articles, poetry and travel writing – reflects a passion I have always engendered for the natural world. The book contains both works of my imagination and factual pieces. Many of these articles and short stories are about the wonders of nature found in Wales.

You will find here pieces on peregrine falcons, erudite naturalists, historic coastal walks, and some of the unusual and rarely seen animals you might be lucky enough to encounter in and around the city of Cardiff, where I returned to live in the year 2000. The book also takes the reader to Cornwall, where some years ago I completed a very special cycling journey across the stunning county, observing and recording some of the wonderful places I visited, and some of the fantastic wildlife I was lucky to discover. Another article transports you to a relatively remote part of the Peak District, where my brother and I went in search of Britain's only silk moth: a beautiful, fantastic insect, and a true emperor both in name and in nature.

You will discover short stories, poetry and articles about fish and fishing, some based on personal experience, others, works of my imagination and observations. You will find, if you care to look, ghost stories and haunting tales of both fish and fishermen; some, darkly comic, others, perhaps a little scary. Another story takes you to the tropical seas, and the plight of our troubled oceans and planet, a subject very close to my heart. You will also discover here, the world of the sea lamprey: a rare, protected, and somewhat gruesome fish that has been on our earth since before the age of the dinosaurs.

Nature has its own rhythms, some of which I hope to have interpreted in this book. I hope that you, the reader, will discover some of those rhythms for yourself, but, most of all, that you gain some pleasure and enjoyment from the words I have written.

I feel we should all continue to dream at any age, and that perhaps, in some small way, you too can join me in those dreams.

Enjoy.

TRAVEL WRITING

CORNISH TIME

I was told the locals called it 'Cornish time'. I guess it was a sense of not knowing what day it was, or even what time it was, and in that sense, the passage of time in such stunning surroundings really had little meaning.

I was on holiday, approaching my fiftieth birthday, and about to spend seven days walking and cycling around the southern coast of Cornwall. I would cycle one hundred and thirty miles in all, and walk another twenty. I would cycle up and down many hills, get lost a few times, and be knocked from my bike into a ditch as a huge articulated lorry roared past me on a quiet country road, sweeping me into a tangle of nettles and brambles. But with only injured pride and a few sharp pricks and stings to contend with, I would soon recover. And a few days into my journey, as I relaxed in the beautiful village of Gorran Haven, four miles south of the Lost Gardens of Heligan, I would experience what it really meant to become one with 'Cornish time'.

I arrived in Penzance, by train, at the beginning of August 2012. I'd left my home city of Cardiff some five hours earlier, locking my mountain bike in the carriage close to my seat. After studying my map closely, I made the decision to cycle towards the Lizard Peninsula where I hoped to find accommodation for the night. It was great to be on my bike again and in the open air after the somewhat claustrophobic confines of the train. The cycling was easy as I left Penzance. I passed St Michael's Mount whilst following the coastal path for a few miles, before the terrain became more difficult as I approached the town of Helston. I'd been forewarned about the very hilly nature of southern Cornwall; a fact that became increasingly apparent as my journey progressed! So, it was quite refreshing to come across one of the few flat areas of my trip on the A3083, which bisects the Royal Naval Base at Culdrose.

By the time I arrived in the village of Lizard in the early evening, some four hours and twenty-seven miles after leaving Penzance, I was rather hot and quite tired. I was looking for somewhere to stay for the night, and eventually found the Housel Bay Hotel. The hotel is the most southerly located hotel in Britain and a fine example of late Victorian architecture, built in the early 1880s with the approval of the then prime minister, William Gladstone. The Cornish Coastal Path runs through the hotel gardens and provides access to some of the most magnificent locations on the British mainland. With a near perfect position on Lizard Point, the Housel Bay Hotel overlooks the western approaches of the Atlantic Ocean, where it meets the English Channel. Guests are able to relax, watching the endless procession of ships leaving the Channel, or enjoying glimpses of sandy Housel Bay Cove, nestling just beneath the cliff at the front of the hotel. I couldn't quite believe just how beautiful my location was. After some much-needed food and a couple of pints of Cornish Rattler – a cider made at the St Austell Brewery – I fell blissfully asleep in my room.

Sometime during the night I was awoken by what I assumed to be thunder and lightning. The rain was hammering against my window as the wind lashed the storm against the glass. I sat up in bed, rubbing my bleary eyes, before peering outside into the darkness. I was amazed to see that the flash of light came not from any bolt of lightning, but from the twin towers of the Lizard Lighthouse, perhaps half a mile from the hotel. For some time, I was transfixed. A lighthouse flashing eerie signals through my bedroom window in the middle of the night; what more could a man want from a holiday in such stunning surroundings! Eventually, I drifted wearily back into a dream-filled sleep. Ghostly galleons, the benign spirits of drowned sailors, and long dead smugglers were to dominate those dreams.

I awoke early the next day, showered, then made my way downstairs. The previous night's storm had abated and now it was a wonderfully sunny August morning. I sat in the breakfast lounge of the hotel, enjoying my cooked meal of locally sourced produce and absorbing the heat of the summer sun, which had already warmed the interior of the building. The view from the lounge was magnificent. Beyond the hotel gardens the waters of Housel Bay Cove shimmered with a turquoise iridescence, whilst the golden sands of the beach would not seem out of place on any tropical island.

After breakfast, and on the advice of the hotel proprietor, I decided to walk the South West Coastal Path to Kynance Cove; a round trip of about eight miles. It was not possible to cycle this section of the coastal path and, indeed, cycling is banned from most of its length as apart from the often precarious footpaths, much of the path has populations of rare plants and animals, and these unique habitats could be destroyed by the actions of cyclists. In fact, the hotel and its adjoining gardens are part of a Special Area of Conservation, and today I was really hoping to see one of the iconic animals which so typified the wildness of this area of Cornwall. One of which was a magnificent black bird with a bright red beak: the chough. A member of the crow family, the bird had recolonised the rocky coastline in tiny numbers from the continent, and was now nesting and breeding amongst the cliffs. I set off from the hotel just after nine o'clock that morning with a camera, a good pair of binoculars, and a rucksack containing the day's essentials.

My walk to Kynance Cove varied in degrees of difficulty. At times I was quite close to the cliff edge, but there were many flat sections of the coastal path, well away from any precipitous drops. And, indeed, the flatter sections of the path could be accessed by those both young and old alike. I walked for about four hours, passing Lizard Point and the lighthouse which had flashed those eerie signals into my bedroom the previous night. The lighthouse is now a heritage centre. I also encountered the 'most southerly house in the British Isles', the now defunct lifeboat station, a cafe, and a gift shop. The gift shop sold various ornaments fashioned from serpentine rock, the rock from which much of the coastal landscape is constructed. In places where the path fell sharply away to the sea, it was very narrow, winding up those rugged cliffs like a snake.

On the flatter sections of the path, further away from the cliff edge, I chatted to some of the walkers I met. A couple sitting on a bench, who must have been well into their eighties, told me as they stared out to sea, 'We will remember this view for the rest of our lives'. I could hardly have disagreed, and as I peered down from the clifftop and into the sea I spotted the whiskery faces of a pair of grey seals, their inquisitive heads bobbing up and down in the swell like wine corks. A kestrel hovered above me, perhaps only fifty feet from where I stood, using the strong onshore winds to help it hover as it hunted for prey in the grass below.

As the summer sun beat down from the cloudless sky, I was optimistic that it would not be long before I saw a chough. The next bird I saw however, was a pied flycatcher, a small black and white bird which darted between the grass stems in search of insects. I also encountered other creatures, including a millipede crawling along the footpath, and one of the largest species of British butterfly, a member of the fritillary family. It was difficult to tell if the butterfly was a dark green fritillary or a silver-washed fritillary, but it was obvious from the sheer size and brilliant colours of the insect that it was one of these majestic giants. It was a special sighting for me.

It was soon after this that I saw my target species: the chough. It was great to see one in Britain, and it was wonderful to see that these black crows with distinctive, downturned beaks had returned to this stretch of the Cornish coastline. I didn't even need my binoculars to view the bird as it perched on a windswept clifftop, some one hundred feet from where I stood. Although with the aid of those binoculars, the view of the bird, and in particular its bright red beak, was all the more spectacular. For what seemed an age, it remained on the cliff edge, before flying off into the distance and disappearing over the sea. The sighting of the chough had made my day; anything else I saw now would just be a bonus.

Soon after, I arrived at Kynance Cove. There were already many people on the beach, including a number of surfers. This spot, with its swathe of golden sands and cafe, was very attractive and family friendly; but to some extent, I had come to Cornwall to get away from people, so I decided not to stay long. I began my return journey to the hotel satisfied with what I had seen that day. The views had been stunning, the wildlife wonderful. That night, after some food and a couple of pints of Cornish Rattler, I drifted into a deep sleep. Outside, the lights from the Lizard Lighthouse permeated the blackness of the still Cornish night.

I awoke early the next morning. The weather was fine, and the skies azure blue. It wasn't a difficult decision to spend a second day on the Lizard Peninsula, and a second night in the Housel Bay Hotel. After another delicious cooked breakfast, I thought I might take a leisurely walk into the village of Lizard itself. The previous day, on my clifftop walk to Kynance Cove, one of the locals had told me about the possible location of some adders. He'd seen a nest of them, close to a five-bar gate on one of the footpaths which leads inland from the clifftops to the village. He'd also told me that one of the female adders was pregnant, and that it was the biggest and fattest adder he'd ever seen! Sadly, in spite of my best efforts, I could not locate the gate, nor the adders.

The village of Lizard is very pleasant, with a village green and quaint shops which cater for tourists, but not in the tacky, tasteless way that some places do. One of the local treats, which I would recommend anyone trying, was Roskilly's ice cream which comes in all manner of unusual flavours. I had a daily craving for this ice cream, and downed many cornets throughout my journey across Cornwall, in the main because I was often hot and dehydrated from either cycling or walking, and the cornets had the much-desired effect of cooling me down. Although I must say, I never really needed an excuse to eat ice cream. Roskilly's was one of the best ice creams I had ever tasted, and it was a pleasure to experiment with the different flavours! After eating a pasty – of course I had to try one – I took a leisurely stroll back to the hotel, along the coastal path.

I had decided to take it a little easier today, so I thought I'd cycle to the traditional fishing port of Cadgwith, a relatively short distance of some eight miles from the hotel. The descent into Cadgwith is quite steep, but the village itself is absolutely stunning with picture-postcard views. As I sat on the harbour wall, staring down into the translucent, shallow sea, I became transfixed by the small shoals of fish which glinted like jewels in the golden sunlight. A number of traditional fishing boats were moored on the stony beach. Cottages and houses, some with thatched roofs, and magnificent flower-filled gardens gave Cadgwith that chocolate-box image of quaintness that I for one was more than happy to embrace. It was not difficult to imagine those traditional fishing boats tilting and riding on the 'fishingboat-bobbing sea' as the tide came in, just like the line from that famous Dylan Thomas play, Under Milk Wood.

Later on, after wandering the leafy lanes, exploring some of the shops and an art gallery which promoted the work of local artists, I cycled back up the hill and returned to the hotel. That evening I sat in the hotel gardens, enjoying some sandwiches while watching the sun go down and the light fade across the sea. As my mind drifted with the clouds, I sensed that I could have stayed in the area for another week, such was the beauty and magnificence of the Lizard's wonderful coastline, but for my journey's sake, I knew that I had to move on. I would check out the next day and head for Falmouth.

I vacated the hotel the following morning; I had a real feeling of sadness to be leaving such a beautiful area behind. Without doubt, staying at the Housel Bay Hotel was a wonderful experience, and I would recommend it to anyone. I knew that I would return to stay at the hotel in the years to come, to spend more time walking and exploring the magnificent Lizard coastline. I was heading for the Helford River, where I'd put my bike on the ferry, and cross the river in the direction of Falmouth.

My journey was pleasant with clear, sunny blue skies. I arrived at Helford Passage in the early afternoon, having crossed the sparse heathland of Goonhilly Downs – a site made famous by the huge satellite dishes of the Earth Station which are visible for miles. The Downs are part of a Site of Special Scientific Interest, where adders and stonechats are common. The raised plateau on which the Downs sit was also one of the few flat areas I had cycled across since leaving Penzance. I can say, without equivocation, that this flat, straight road was welcome relief for both mind and body alike!

The heathland is also home to many rare plants, including the Cornish Heath, which has been adopted as the county flower. A welcome light shower accompanied me as I left the sparse landscape of the Downs behind. Some three hours later, I was making the steep and snake-like descent into Helford Passage; the brakes on my mountain bike were tested to their limit.

As I crossed a small ford, which spanned the river at one of its narrowest points, one of the locals ushered me in the direction of a jetty from which the ferry departed. I had no idea what time the ferry left, and I was a bit dismayed to arrive at the jetty just at the point when the boat (which was little more than a small river cruiser) was leaving for the opposite riverbank! I had missed the crossing by minutes, and would now have to wait for a further three hours for the tide to turn and the ferry to come back.

On the upside, I now had plenty of time to explore my surroundings. Having locked my bike to some railings, I wandered up and down the riverbank, turning over stones and exploring the myriad rock pools in the hope of discovering some rare marine creature, with all the enthusiasm of a seven-year-old child. As in most years gone by, all I really found were a few prawns, a crab or two, and the odd dead mussel. Still, it was great to feel like a child again, even if I hadn't found the remains of a giant squid, or some yet to be discovered prehistoric monster!

After indulging in some inquisitive rock pooling, I headed to a local pub, where I ate locally caught crab and seasonal salad sandwiches. After that wonderful lunch, I cycled back to the jetty to await the ferry's return. As I lay on the slipway, using my rucksack for a pillow, the August sun lulled me into a light, dreamy sleep. Some time later, I awoke to the sight of the small ferry chugging its way across the estuary. As the boat pulled up alongside the jetty, the helmswoman explained to me that it was fine to put my bike on her small craft. In only a matter of minutes I was on the other side of the Helford River, and cycling up a steep hill in the direction of Falmouth.

It had taken me three hours to cycle the twenty-eight miles from the Housel Bay Hotel to what seemed a veritable metropolis! My journey from the most southerly point in the British Isles, the Lizard, had taken me up and down many hills, so after cycling around Falmouth for a while, and really feeling quite fatigued, I booked myself into a rather basic B&B. I calculated that at this point, since getting off the train in Penzance, I had cycled a total of sixty-four miles and walked more than ten in the vicinity of the Lizard Peninsula. I was grateful for a rest, hot coffee and a shower, and although the hotel was nothing like the luxurious Housel Bay Hotel, it was clean and tidy, and that was all that really mattered.

After a brief nap in my room, I took a leisurely stroll into the centre of Falmouth. I explored the waterfront, admiring the myriad ships of all shapes and sizes, including a number of small warships anchored in the harbour. I sat on the quayside, where I enjoyed a Chinese takeaway. It was early evening before I returned to my hotel. It was only when I switched on the television in my room that I realised that I had not used any technology for three days, and had almost forgotten that the London Olympics were taking place. But to me, that act of not switching on the television was really what 'Cornish time' was all about. I was losing myself in other, more valuable pursuits.

I fell asleep on my bed, just after Usain Bolt streaked to victory in the one hundred metres. It turned out to be a truly great spectacle, and despite my break from technology, I must admit that I was secretly quite glad that I had witnessed such a momentous event.

The following day, I woke early and made my way to the quayside in Falmouth, where I booked myself and my bike on the ferry for the crossing across the Fal River, to the picturesque village of St Mawes. There is only one road out of St Mawes which, of course, is up a very steep hill! The weather remained good with intermittent clear blue skies, interspersed with occasional cotton-wool cumulus clouds.

Although a light breeze accompanied me on my journey, I soon worked up a sweat as I followed the A3078 a mile or two inland from the coast in a north-easterly direction towards Veryan Green. This was marked on my map as another picturesque village. I then joined National Cycle Route three, after cycling a distance of some ten miles from St Mawes. My journey was quite arduous at times, with the constant cycling up and down hills taking its toll. I was longing for some continuous straight, flat road which stretched for some distance over the horizon. But I concluded that, with me being so close to the coast, and this being Cornwall, this scenario was about as likely as me winning the Tour de France!

I still had no idea where I would end up that day, and in total I would cycle twenty-six miles before I found my accommodation for the night. Again, the views I encountered from all of the coves were absolutely stunning, which more than compensated for the fatigue that was now creeping into my legs. I was often hypnotised by the tranquil, turquoise-blue waters which lapped against the golden sands of many of these secret little bays. And, to top it all, as I got off my bike for a rest and to take in another of these wonderful views, I was to glimpse the form of particularly rare and rather plump lizard scuttling across the road in front of me. The view of this lizard became another really important sighting for me as, having seen many smaller common lizards before, I was positive that I had just encountered a beautiful and scarce sand lizard. This was another first for me, and although my sighting had been fleeting, I was thrilled to have seen one of Britain's most colourful and exquisite reptiles!

Four hours after leaving Falmouth, I found myself cycling down the steep descent into the stunning coastal village of Gorran Haven. Up to this point in my journey, I had cycled ninety miles and walked a further ten miles along the rugged paths of the Lizard Peninsula. Despite drinking plenty of water, I was quite dehydrated and ready for a rest as I booked myself into another picturesque B&B in my eventful trek across southern Cornwall.

Having replenished myself with copious amounts of fluids, the owners of the small hotel told me a tale of a German couple who had stayed with them in a previous year, and were cycling south towards Land's End. How far the couple had cycled to get to Gorran Haven, the proprietor of the hotel could not remember, but what he did say was that the couple had become really quite ill, having clearly underestimated the difficulties of the steep, undulating landscape of this part of England. He said that the couple had no choice but to stay at the hotel for two days, until they rehydrated themselves and recovered their strength and resolve to continue on their journey. I could certainly understand why!

That night, I wandered in the direction of the beach, and to the only chip shop in the village – a chip shop that was so busy with locals and holidaymakers alike that it always ran out of fish by eight o'clock, and was forced to close at this time every night. And I could see why; I would have to say that these were some of the best fish and chips I had ever tasted. After enjoying my meal, whilst sitting on the quayside and watching the sun set over the sea, I took a short, leisurely walk to the top of the cliffs, overlooking the bay. As I sat quietly on a bench, absorbing the sounds and scents of the gathering dusk, a mixed flock of swallows, house martins and swifts trawled the sky for insects only feet above my head. Below me the small sandy cove had emptied of human life, and my thoughts turned to a poem I had written about swallows some years before. It is a favourite poem of mine, and one which seemed to encapsulate the scene above me to a tee.

Swallows

Like darting fish
flashing in the shallows
they trawl the slack,
swallows.

They come in waves
with fins for wings
to fish the ocean sky;
trawl the slack –
suck their minnows dry.

'Cornish time' had swallowed me up, and I was so grateful that it had. Time, and the days of the week, had become an irrelevance, and that made me happy and content. I was in a tranquil place as I approached my fiftieth birthday.

The next day, I woke to the sounds of cows lowing somewhere in the distance of the mist-shrouded morning. Nesting herring gulls scratched and scuttled about the roof above me. Today I would cycle four miles south to the Lost Gardens of Heligan.

The gardens were magnificent! And when the sun appeared from behind the clouds it made my visit to Heligan all the more breathtaking. It was a place I would recommend to anyone, with ample parking space and a visitor centre which caters for all age groups. There were hides overlooking ponds where you could observe all manner of aquatic and non-aquatic animal life; they also included many interactive tools which would appeal to children and adults alike. There were herb gardens and a wonderful variety of trees and shrubs from all corners of the world; including specialist growing areas where rare plants from countries such as New Zealand flourished in the temperate climate.

It was wonderful to discover large ponds where beautiful red-finned roach and rudd swam in huge shoals, surrounded on the banks by great ferns and lush, luxuriant water-loving plants. In the shimmering heat the roach and rudd seemed to hover just below the water's surface, like an armada of miniature submarines; they were completely at peace and in tune with the serenity of their world.

I was loath to leave the ponds as they had a soothing, hypnotic effect on me and let my imagination run away with itself. But I knew I had to move on, so after walking through the depression known as the Lost Valley, I wound my way back towards the visitor centre to enjoy an ice cream and a brief meander around the shop. Half an hour later I was cycling northwards towards St Austell.

My initial thoughts on arriving in St Austell were that I would stay in a B&B and visit the Eden Project; but in the end I decided to cycle onwards in the direction of Fowey, a place that had been recommended to me by the owner of the last guesthouse in which I'd stayed. As usual, there were many undulating hills on my cycle to Fowey. By the time I arrived, some twenty-two miles after leaving Gorran Haven, I was feeling fatigued and once again, despite my best efforts, I was really quite dehydrated. The cumulative effect of almost a week's hard cycling and walking was beginning to take its toll on me.

As I descended the steep incline into Fowey, I came across a very attractive-looking B&B, with numerous flower-filled hanging baskets adorning the building's walls. The owner of the premises informed me he had a room for one night, perhaps two. I asked him if he had anywhere safe I could lock my bike. I'll remember what he said to me for a very long time!

'Oh, you don't need to lock your bike! No one is going to nick a bike in Fowey! They might nick a boat, but not a bike!'

My reply, in my somewhat rather exhausted, dehydrated state went something along these lines: 'No one is bloody likely to nick a bike anywhere along the bloody southern coast of Cornwall! There's too many damn hills!'

He was a large, rather rotund man, not dissimilar to a bearded Brian Blessed, and his raucous, bellowing laughter merely seemed to confirm my assertion that he thought I was a little mad for cycling all the miles that I had. I pushed my bike into an old outhouse for safekeeping (where it remained unlocked) and retired to my room. After a short rest, I decided that I would be staying in Fowey for two nights. I knew that tomorrow there would be no cycling for me. My mind and body were telling me that I needed a good rest, and that's just the way it was to be.

That night, after a pub meal and a brief look around the shops and harbour, I lay on my bed to watch more of the Olympics on the television. I'm proud to say that I witnessed Mo Farah scorch to victory in the five thousand metres. London and the Olympics seemed a million miles away, but once again I was glad that I was able to witness more from such a remarkable event.

Although the decision to stay two nights in Fowey was really made for me by the levels of fatigue I now felt, Fowey was such a lovely, picturesque port that I was grateful to be able to spend some time exploring the town on foot.

The next morning, I headed off towards the centre of town. It was great to amble through the streets, leafing through the second-hand bookshops, and wandering the art galleries full of work by local artists. After a while, I came across an old, rather dilapidated building close to the quayside, which I was very pleased to see housed the Fowey Aquarium. I decided to visit, and it was very enjoyable to observe the range of marine life, both large and small, patrolling their tanks. This marine life included both lobsters and pollack; some of the pollack were close to ten pounds in weight.

I felt like a kid in a sweet shop again! I was taken to a world of wave-swept rock pools where mini beasts, including crabs, gobies and blennies, darted between translucent prawns and shrimps which frolicked in their environment as if they were in the open ocean.

Chatting to the owner of the aquarium, it was wonderful to hear that once the fish had grown too big for their tanks, local fisherman would return them to the sea where they might grow into real giants. The fish would then be replaced by freshly caught smaller members of the same species. This was to be the case with the ten-pound pollack, which were about to be returned to the ocean from whence they came. It was great to see that people actually cared about the creatures in their charge, and that the animals weren't just there as moneymaking exhibits.

After reluctantly leaving the aquarium, I wandered the side streets of Fowey. As I walked along the main street, I was amazed to see a man motoring gingerly towards me in an electric wheelchair, accompanied by what I could only assume were his elderly parents, and a pair of parrots! Yes, parrots! Each exquisitely feathered bird was tethered loosely to his shoulders. At first I thought I was seeing things. But having spoken to the man, I learnt of his affection for his birds. He could not bear to leave them at home, so he had brought them on holiday with him and was now simply taking them for a walk! This made me think of my two rescue cats, Chi-Chi and I-Ching, which I had left incarcerated in a cattery near Cardiff. It was their first time in a cattery, and they were very nervous; and seeing the parrots made me realise just how much I was missing them. I knew now that it was time to return to Cardiff.

That night, I wandered the quayside of Fowey, enjoying a pint, some great food, and some people-watching. Later on, to the background noise of more triumphs at the London Olympics, I drifted off to sleep.

In the morning, I checked out from the hotel and crossed the Fowey estuary by ferry to the picturesque village of Polruan, before climbing the hill in a north-easterly direction towards Liskeard, where I would catch the train back to Cardiff.

It rained steadily for the whole of the sixteen-mile journey to Liskeard station. This, perhaps, rather fortuitously, was the only day of my seven-day trip when it had rained.

So, considering the dreadfully wet summer we had in 2012, I counted myself incredibly lucky that I had encountered such great weather. In spite of my waterproofs, I was soaked to the skin. As I sank into my seat on the train, I felt tired, yet in some ways truly invigorated.

In my relaxed state of my mind, I reflected on my journey. I had really enjoyed my cycling journey across southern Cornwall. I had cycled one hundred and thirty miles in all, and walked a further twenty miles along the Coastal Path, much of it around the Lizard Peninsula. I had eaten some wonderful food, stayed in some beautiful locations, and seen some magnificent wildlife. Yes, the cycling had at times been hard, and I must have burnt thousands of calories, but I knew that one day I would return to Cornwall and continue my cycling and walking pilgrimage around the stunning county.

Four hours later I would be back in Cardiff. I thought fondly of my two cats and, although I had felt very guilty about putting them in the cattery, I hoped they would be really pleased to see me. As I drifted off into a light sleep, I knew that I would remember my cycling and walking holiday across southern Cornwall for the rest of my life.

POSTSCRIPT

My cycling journey across southern Cornwall was really something of a pilgrimage for me. I have always enjoyed cycling, and have cycled thousands of miles over the years. Being on two wheels gives you the freedom of the open roads, and allows you access to the natural world in a way that is in part, lost to those who use motorised transport. I must stress that I am not against cars in any way. To some, cars are a necessity, to others, a luxury of vanity. But you sense more of nature when you are cycling or walking, and sometimes nature comes to you, when clearly this would not be the case should you be driving. My cycling journey across southern Cornwall brought me very close to nature.

In some ways, my journey was cathartic. Between 2009 and 2011, I had four knee operations on my left knee, was unable to work, and was registered disabled for two years. I was on crutches for much of this time, had some serious orthopaedic surgery, and was in chronic pain throughout. I never had the best posture as a child, having broken a bone in my right hip in my early teens, which later led to an operation in my early twenties. My posture, I believe, had in some way contributed to the overall deterioration and condition of my knee. Although in some ways, as the surgeon said, I was just unlucky, with one condition developing after another as my knee deteriorated.

On the brighter side, the nurses who treated me said I was bionic! And, of course, as medical professionals, I had to agree with them wholeheartedly! Eventually, I made a full recovery, went back to work, and began to cycle again. So, it was just wonderful for me to visit southern Cornwall, and complete my solo cycle ride. I was well again, and that's all that really mattered.

Perhaps, subconsciously, I had a second reason for cycling across Cornwall. A great uncle of mine, William Best Harris, now deceased, had been city librarian in Plymouth from 1947 until 1974. He wrote a number of books about Devon and Cornwall, many of which are still available to this day.

Uncle Bill spent nearly eight years walking most of the coastline of Devon and Cornwall with his wife Betty, researching details for a weekly broadcast for the BBC radio programme, Morning Sou'West. Honey, their golden Labrador, walked with them – starting the long trek as a puppy and ending it as a middle-aged lady! William Best Harris died in 1987, at the age of seventy-three.

Part of this diary was published in *Explore England* magazine 2016.

IN SEARCH OF EMPERORS

It was early May, and the middle of the week. My brother and I had driven from the village of Chinley in Derbyshire, where I was staying, to the Upper Derwent Valley in the hope of seeing Britain's only silk moth. Not a king, or a queen, but an emperor: Saturnia pavonia to give it its Latin name. A magnificent and beautifully marked insect which occurs throughout the Palearctic region, and is the only member of its family to be found in Britain, where it is appropriately called the emperor moth.

We had driven to South Yorkshire and into the Peak District National Park, an upland area of great diversity which is split into the northern Dark Peak, which is mainly moorland and whose geological foundation is gritstone, and the southern White Peak, which is predominantly limestone. The Peak District National Park lies mainly in northern Derbyshire, but also covers parts of Cheshire, Greater Manchester, Staffordshire, and South and West Yorkshire.

We drove as far as we could into the park, before parking the car within sight of Ladybower Reservoir. We set off on foot, walking steadily uphill, passing Howden Reservoir and along the road which bisected both coniferous and deciduous woodland. We continued until the flora and fauna of the landscape became the peat bog and heather moorland so typical of the habitat of the emperor moth.

A lone fell runner ran past us, panting heavily, tracking his way ever upward between well-worn paths and boulder-strewn streams. Meadow pipits flitted incessantly about, skimming across the top of the heather in search of insects. From over a distant peak the haunting cry of a curlew could be heard. We walked steadily, stopping every so often to scan the heather with binoculars in the hope of seeing an emperor moth. The weather was good, although as we climbed higher, the wind picked up and whistled down the valley.

We were only likely to see the male moth as the female flies mainly by night. The male has a wingspan of some sixty millimetres, whilst the female is somewhat larger, with a wingspan of eighty millimetres. Both male and female moths are extraordinarily beautiful insects. The male has brown and white forewings, marked with red and orange, with bold eyespots designed to deter predators. The hind wings are mainly orange with similar eyespot markings. The female is generally grey and white with eyespots like the male. The male moths have delicate, feathery antennae, which are works of art in themselves.

As we continued to climb, sheep monitored us nervously from a distance. Occasionally they would let us get close, but those with lambs ran off as we approached. Up to this point, at an altitude of some three hundred metres, we were yet to see the insect we had come to the moors to observe. Other creatures made themselves known to us with regularity; red grouse were plentiful on the peaks, their rapid wing beats often startling us as they shot up from the cover of the heather. I had never seen red grouse before today, and their pretty, intricately patterned feathers, which we frequently found trapped amongst the sparse foliage, provided me with an appropriately eco-friendly souvenir of our day out.

Apart from the fell runner, we had hardly seen another human being, likely due to it being midweek and our route not being a recognised walk. So, as we approached the out of season shooting area known for its grouse butts, at an altitude of five hundred metres, I guessed the lack of fellow walkers might increase our chances of seeing more animals.

Indeed, we had a great view of a pair of wheatears, and a stunning view of some stonechats. But our best sighting of the day, thus far, was the sight of a mountain hare leaping from cover, still in its winter coat, only fifty metres in front of us. Neither my brother nor I had ever seen a mountain hare before, so we were really pleased to see this remarkable animal, which had been reintroduced to the Peak District back in the late nineteenth century.

It was now mid-afternoon, and although it was blowing a gale on the top of the Dark Peak, the weather remained dry and we stopped for a spot of lunch, seeking shelter in a small depression in the ground. Some three hours after we left the car, close to Ladybower Reservoir, we began to descend from the top of the mountain.

As we snaked our way downhill, in the shelter of the valleys, the wind dropped and the early May sunshine provided a welcome relief from the gale we had experienced higher up. It was then that we saw our first emperor moth, then the second, then the third, and then the fourth. We did not get too close to our quarry, but with good binoculars, we were able to positively identify the fast flying insects as male emperor moths.

Our walk had been a success; not only had we found the stunning insect we had always longed to see, we had observed animals unique to England and the Peak District National Park. As we took our walking boots off, to sit quietly in the car and reflect on the day's events, we had a great view of a woodcock, sitting on the grass verge only metres from our vehicle. Thinking it must have been injured – because we were so close and it had remained motionless – I approached the animal, only to watch it fly off into the forest, a truly healthy bird.

I was over the moon with all the animals we had seen that day, particularly the encounter with the mountain hare and, of course, our audience with royalty: a true emperor of its domain, a majestic and beautifully marked insect, and a stunning moth so typical of the upland heather moors of the Peak District National Park. It had been a wonderful day out, and a walk I would treasure for a long time.

This article was previously published in *Evergreen Magazine*.

THE HIDDEN GEMS OF BARRY ISLAND

When you think of Barry Island, I'm sure your first thoughts are of funfairs, amusement arcades and overcrowded, sandy beaches. But if you look closely, behind this facade, you'll soon discover some wonderful walks, a fascinating history, and some real treasures of the natural world.

Barry Island, named after the sixth-century Saint Baruc, forms part of the town of Barry in the Vale of Glamorgan. What is now a peninsula was in fact an island until the 1880s, when it was linked to the mainland as the town of Barry increased in size. This, in part, was due to the opening of Barry Dock by the Barry Dock Railway Company. Barry's stretch of coastline on the Bristol Channel has the world's second highest tidal range of fifteen metres, or forty-nine feet, second only to that of the Bay of Fundy in eastern Canada. The tidal range, as an occasional fisherman, is something of which I am acutely aware.

In July 2015, my friend and I caught a train from Cardiff, with the intention of fishing from the rocks at Barry Island. Although it was a warm, sunny day, fishing with light tackle, as we intended, proved practically impossible as the wind whipped the waves into white horses, throwing them against the rocks. With little weight on our lines, we were simply unable to cast into that wind, which was blowing a gale. Still, if we couldn't fish, we could always walk. And as both myself and my friend were interested in all aspects of the natural world, we thought we'd start by walking the concrete path above the beach at Barry Island (Whitmore Bay), in the direction of Jackson's Bay. Jackson's Bay, with its golden sands, secluded nature, and pleasant views must surely be one of Barry's best kept secrets.

As we walked, we discussed the six-foot-long swordfish which was found washed up on the beach below us in 2008, and although we had no expectation of finding such a rarity, we hoped we might discover other unusual animals or plants. We were both members of Butterfly Conservation and were always on the lookout for an unusual butterfly or moth. We were keenly aware that there was always the possibility of the sighting of a migrant hummingbird hawkmoth, or a clouded yellow. Suffice to say that we saw neither of these majestic insects, but we did discover several colonies of small blue butterflies, Britain's smallest butterfly, and now something of a relative rarity. I marvelled at the tenacity of these tiny insects – whose forewings were almost black, or dark brown, with a dusting of blue – as they flitted from flower to flower, barely flying more than a foot above the sparse coastal vegetation, which was their shield and sanctuary from the powerful winds which blew off the sea. To me, for such tiny butterflies, their struggle for survival in such adverse weather conditions bordered on the truly heroic!

We continued to walk the concrete footpath, below the coastal lookout station at Nell's Point and in the direction of Jackson's Bay. Natural springs above the cliffs had worn away holes in the softer rocks below, and pools of freshwater gathered at the cliff base. Above, from the tangle of foliage which strangled the cliff face, came the clap of a wood pigeon's wings, accompanied by the melodious voice of a song thrush.

Looking out to sea, in the direction of North Devon, the islands of Flat Holm and Steep Holm dominated the Bristol Channel. A number of years ago, I spent a long adventure weekend on the island of Flat Holm. It is an island well worth a visit, with some unique flora and fauna, and a history that goes back thousands of years. The island can be accessed from Cardiff, or Weston-super-Mare, via a daily boat trip, and visitors can spend up to six hours on Flat Holm enjoying a great day out.

In the foliage at the base of the cliffs, I spotted a nest (tent) of what was probably once home to some small tortoiseshell caterpillars. The web-like structure had long since been vacated by the caterpillars, but the tent had survived the worst the elements could throw at it, and so too hopefully, had most of the caterpillars.

As we approached the secluded, golden sands of Jackson's Bay, I spotted the distinctive purple flowers of deadly nightshade, or Belladona as it is also known, sheltering amongst the other plants at the base of the cliff. The plant, a member of the tomato family, is highly toxic to humans, so must not be touched under any circumstances. The consumption of just a small number of berries can prove fatal. Nevertheless, it was very interesting to observe such a toxic but important plant for wildlife in its natural environment. In spite of the toxicity of the berries, animals do eat them, finding them sweet, and dispersing the seeds of the plant in their droppings.

As my friend and I came to the end of our walk, and we clambered down onto the golden sands of Jackson's Bay, we had almost forgotten about fishing. In spite of the wind we had really enjoyed our short journey, which was barely a mile from the funfairs and amusement arcades so often associated with Barry Island.

Yes, Barry Island has far more to offer than the superficial; there are some wonderful animals, plants, and secret places to discover. Take my advice, and look beyond the hustle and bustle. You never know what you might find.

POSTSCRIPT

If you were to take a different route, and travel in the opposite direction from Barry Island's Whitmore Beach, I would recommend walking to the headland at Friar's Point. The headland is one of the best examples of calcareous, cowslip-dominated hay meadow in South East Wales, and is an area of Special Scientific Interest. It is the home to a variety of butterflies, bees, grasshoppers and other insects. It is an area where I myself have spotted another relative insect rarity: the grizzled skipper, a small and pretty, almost speckled butterfly. Sadly, this species is struggling to survive in many of its old habitats across Britain, but it's presence here amongst the wildflowers on the grassy headland is very welcome.

The headland is also home to a medieval pillow mound where rabbits were kept in medieval times and bred as an important food source. And if you continue onwards, walking to the end of the track, before turning right, you will come across the old harbour, with its share of rusting hulks and a history going back centuries. But, then, perhaps that history is for another day.

This article was published in *Evergreen Magazine.*

IN MEMORY OF MARY GILLHAM, MBE

I felt a strong affinity with Mary Gillham. I'd spent many years cycling and walking the Taff Trail – a Sustrans cycle route which stretches some fifty-five miles from Cardiff to Brecon – observing, recording and writing about the wildlife of the area.

Indeed, I had actually cycled the whole route itself some years before, but had also spent many happy hours in the last sixteen years exploring my local patch, Forest Farm Country Park, which Mary, as a naturalist and writer herself, had got to know so well.

Forest Farm Country Park lies approximately five miles north of Cardiff, and is only a short distance from where I live. The country park encompasses a designated nature reserve, sections of Glamorgan Canal, and a Site of Special Scientific Interest (Long Wood).

Long Wood is a semi-natural ancient woodland, and the designated nature reserve contains a variety of habitats which include wetlands, open water and semi-improved grassland. Two bird hides overlook the wetlands, and an artificial sand martin cliff has been built near one of the hides. I have also personally observed birds as diverse as water rail and snipe, and bittern have also been seen in recent years. A heronry has also become established on a nearby site, and if you walk along the canal on any warm, sunny day, you'll encounter all sorts of insect and aquatic life.

But now, a bit more about Mary Gillham. Dr Mary Gillham, MBE, dedicated herself to wildlife, and was the founding member of the Glamorgan Naturalists' Trust and the Cardiff Naturalists' Society. She gained a degree in agriculture, a first-class honours in botany and completed a PhD on Skokholm Island. One of the highlights of a truly memorable career included being one of the first women to join an Antarctic expedition in 1959. She was also involved in saving a remote coral island from development, thus preserving its rare and exotic wildlife for posterity. She lectured all over the world in universities as far apart as New Zealand, Australia, Nigeria and England, and also worked in the Adult Education Department of University College Cardiff, until her retirement in 1988.

In her younger days, Mary hitch-hiked her way across South Africa and visited the Americas and central Africa, as well as islands in the Indian Ocean where she led groups of naturalists and was involved in many research projects. In World War Two she volunteered for the Women's Land Army.

So clearly, although I had considerable admiration for Mary's many exploits around the world, and had even travelled and explored some of the more remote areas of Europe myself, it was really our mutual love of the ecology of South East Wales, and in particular, Forest Farm Country Park, which drew me to her.

A recently converted barn, close to the warden's centre in the country park, has been turned into a hide. The hide now overlooks a number of ponds and a small orchard which attracts all manner of wildlife, including grass snakes, slow worms and many species of birds and insects. It really is a beautiful spot, and has quite rightly been named in honour of Mary Gillham, being designated 'The Mary Gillham Memorial Fields'. A quote inside the hide, alluding to Mary herself, 'Inspiring the next generation of naturalists', seemed to sum her up in a nutshell.

Nearby, an eighteenth-century farmhouse has been converted into a conservation centre for the site, which is also now home to the British Trust for Conservation Volunteers (BCTV). The warden's centre also serves as a base for the Cardiff Council Countryside Wardens Team, and is used as an educational environmental resource to nurture an interest and healthy regard for nature amongst schools and special interest groups. The former tree nursery is now a woodland recycling centre, converting fallen or storm-damaged trees into woodchip and park furniture.

Dr Mary Gillham, MBE, died on the 24 March 2013, aged ninety-one. She was awarded the MBE for services to nature conservation in South Wales in 2008. Perhaps it was fitting that her last home was in Radyr, not far from Forest Farm Country Park, and close to the area she knew so well.

She very reluctantly had to sell her beloved cottage at the base of Garth Mountain, Gwaelod-y-Garth, where she'd lived for many years, and move to a flat, as she finally admitted that for such an active person, she was slowing down. And yes; she was still 'Inspiring the next generation of naturalists'. Although I'd never met Mary, I'd like to think I was one of those naturalists.

If you can, just take a moment to sit in the hide overlooking the Mary Gillham Memorial Fields; it's truly a beautiful place. If you can't do that, maybe seek out and read one of her many books. Mary wrote eloquently and passionately about so many aspects of the natural world. She is a lady who deserves to be remembered.

For those interested in reading some of Mary's work, here is a short bibliography of just some of her books:

1963, *Instructions to Young Ornithologists IV: Seabirds*. London: Museum Press.
1966, *A Naturalist in New Zealand*. London: Museum Press.

1967, *Sub-Antarctic Sanctuary: Summertime on Macquarie Island.* London: Victor Gollancz. Perkins, J., Evans, J. and Gillham, M. (1982) The Historic Taf Valleys, Volume 2: In the Brecon Beacons National Park. Cowbridge: D Brown and Sons.
1998, *Town Bred, Country Nurtured: A Naturalist Looks Back Fifty Years.* Cardiff: Gillham, M.
2000, *Islands of the Trade Winds: An Indian Ocean Odyssey.* London: Minerva Press.
2004, *A Natural History of Cardiff.* Wales: Dinefwr Publishers ltd.
2009, *Wildlife Watching in the Slow Lane.* Somerset: Halsgrove.

This article was published in *Evergreen Magazine.*

THE PEREGRINE DIARIES

I first became involved with the RSPB as a volunteer in 2008, after the dramatic rescue of a peregrine falcon chick on the lawns in front of Cardiff's Civic Centre. I was working on the night bus, a refurbished double-decker which served tea, coffee and sandwiches to homeless people on the streets. It was a warm, dry June evening and my first shift on the bus, which was parked outside the steps of the National Museum of Wales.

At approximately half past eight, as everyone began to disperse for the night, I noticed a commotion on the grass some distance away. A young woman, who we later discovered to be a zoology student, was chasing a large bird across the lawns, trying her best to throw her cardigan over the creature. The bird had been hit by a car. Being an enthusiastic, if somewhat amateur ornithologist, I presumed the creature to be one of the gulls that wheeled and soared in the city's skies throughout the day. After the bird – which was in fact a juvenile peregrine falcon and was being mobbed by a number of these gulls – was finally caught, we telephoned the RSPCA and waited for rescue. The peregrine was wrapped in the cardigan and a homeless person took charge, cradling the youngster in one arm like a babe in swaddling clothes. From time to time we checked on its progress, making sure the needle-sharp beak and talons were kept well away from human flesh. Its dark, liquid eyes seemed to transfix us all. The peregrine remained remarkably calm throughout its ordeal.

At ten o'clock an RSPCA van arrived with a film crew. They were from the television programme Animal Rescue 24/7, and as filming continued, the juvenile was duly examined and placed in a cage for transportation.

A few days later, I was really pleased to find that the chick, a female, was unharmed. It was ringed for identification purposes, and soon to be released from the top of city hall, close to where its parents were nesting. To me, there were a few stars to the show: the zoologist who initially caught the chick, the homeless people who cared for it so tenderly, and, of course, the peregrine herself.

A week later, I contacted the RSPB at their Cardiff headquarters in Sutherland House and volunteered for the 'Aren't Birds Brilliant' project, since renamed 'A Date with Nature', which was being run in conjunction with the National Museum of Wales. Volunteering involved showing people the peregrines on Cardiff's City Hall clock tower, and promoting the principles of the RSPB.

The chicks had hatched in early May as tiny balls of fluff. Their parents had commandeered an old raven's nest, just above the clock, which faced south towards Cardiff Bay. Three eggs were laid, and the three chicks which hatched seemed to be doing well.

My first shift at the museum began in early July. Immediately, it became obvious that the public's fascination for these birds knew no bounds, some people could scarcely believe that peregrine falcons were actually nesting in a city. Personally, I likened the tower to an urban clifftop with a plentiful supply of food. In rural areas cliffs would be the peregrine's natural home, and wild wood pigeons, or rock doves, their natural food. They had just moved into the city, with a perfect nesting site, and a perfect supply of prey.

The RSPB had a small stand inside the museum from which the birds could be viewed on a webcam. We handed out leaflets, gave out information about the peregrines, and signed up new members. We helped people see the peregrines through telescopes and binoculars from various vantage points outside. There were some great views of the adults and chicks, and people were often in awe of the birds. In good weather, we put up a marquee on the lawns in front of the museum. Sometimes the chicks could be heard calling for food – a shrill, eerie, piercing cry – and the parents would regularly return with a kill.

On one occasion, I watched the female chick through a telescope. When fully grown, the female is a third bigger than the male, enabling her to hunt larger prey, thereby supplying a variety of food to the youngsters throughout the breeding season. And, as this chick was larger than the other two, it was presumed to be female. I marvelled as she hopped and flapped above a ledge, playing with a carcass of what looked like a pigeon. It was almost comical to watch as she moved the body along the ledge for more than half an hour. This was very likely to be the chick that was rescued back in June, so it was wonderful to see that she was doing well.

The peregrine is a formidable hunter, and the dive, or stoop as it is known, has been timed at over two hundred miles per hour, which makes the peregrine the fastest bird in the world. This, along with the predatory, almost regal appearance of the birds had clearly endeared them to the public.

In other cities, pigeons are said to comprise more than forty per cent of the peregrine's diet, and, although songbirds and waders are also predated upon, we had occasional reports of our adult peregrines attacking and killing gulls.

As the project came to a close towards the end of August, both adults and all three chicks were thought to be still alive, although rarely seen together now. And as their nest of sticks began to disintegrate, I began to wonder where the birds, particularly the youngsters, might go. The name peregrine derives from Latin, meaning 'wanderer', and as the birds in the wild can live up to seventeen years, it was anybody's guess where they might end up. If the chicks did not leave the nest of their own accord, it was inevitable that the adults would drive them away as they competed for food.

The peregrine family had become very popular and thousands of people had enjoyed watching them over the summer. They had become a real tourist attraction. I hoped that the adults would return next spring to produce another clutch of peregrine eggs and I hoped to be there as a volunteer again in 2009. I guessed the public would miss the peregrines; I knew I would.

An abridged version of this article was previously published in *The Countryman* magazine.

THE BEAUTY OF BUTE PARK

I had finished another night shift, just after the turn of the year, and was cycling my usual route home, through Cardiff's Bute Park. I had known Bute Park in all seasons, and even now, in the dark depths of a January morning, with the wind howling and the sun barely up, the arboretum had a kind of stark, spectral beauty.

In a few months, many of the trees, now skeletal and devoid of leaves, would begin to flourish again. New growth would transform the park, and the soil in the flower beds, brown and bare in many places, would become a riot of colour. The dark days of winter still held sway, but if the scent of spring was not yet quite in the air, the days were getting imperceptibly lighter and longer.

The history of the area goes back many centuries, and the activities of countless generations of people have moulded the landscape that is now Bute Park. It is far removed from the site which initially attracted those people; the river and the castle were magnets for early settlements. Nowadays, the park is a public place, and a real green gem in the centre of the city. The park is also Grade-1 listed on Cadw's (Welsh heritage) Register of Parks and Gardens of Special Historic Interest.

From about the twelfth century, the land around the epicentres of the castle and river were used for religious purposes, cottage industries and agriculture. In 1766, the Bute Family, who were wealthy landowners, inherited the castle, and from the nineteenth century onwards began to develop the site. The land around the castle was purchased and pleasurable gardens created. The estate's development reflected the burgeoning prosperity and ambition that characterised Cardiff at the time, with architect William Burgess working alongside Andrew Pettigrew to create a landscape that augmented the intricate work on the castle.

In 1947, the Fifth Marquess of Bute gifted both the castle and grounds to the people of Cardiff, and the land became a public park. Today it is a jewel in the city, and a haven for wildlife. It is also a venue for many public events, including the annual visit of the RHS Flower Show.

Bute Park contains within its boundaries a nationally significant tree collection, an education centre, three cafes, and myriad plants to interest the earnest horticulturalist. The park itself covers an area of fifty-six hectares, which is equivalent to seventy-five football pitches. There are many things to do there, with a number of easily navigated trails guiding you through certain activities and topics. The park is a mixture of urban woodland, arboretum, sports pitches and historic landscape.

The area's history reflects the diverse development of Cardiff. There are many important heritage sites to visit including Cardiff Castle, the Gorsedd Stones, the famous animal wall and the site of Blackfriars Friary.

The park's arboretum contains more than three thousand individual tree species which have been catalogued. The site has more champion trees than in any other UK public park, which gives the area great prestige. Champion trees are the tallest and broadest examples of their species found anywhere in Great Britain.

Cycling has always been a great passion of mine and I have cycled through the park on many occasions. I have watched the blue flash of kingfishers as they dart along the dock feeder stream, and have fished that very same stream, catching small fish such as dace, roach, chub and grayling, all of which are an absolute delight to play on a small fly rod. And, of course, being environmentally conscious, I have always made sure the fish are returned to the water in a healthy state. I've regularly watched the activities of dippers and wagtails as they've bobbed up and down on the bank in their differing ways.

Over the years, I have also watched peregrine falcons and buzzards flying high over the area. Bute Park is notable as a breeding ground of the scarce, lesser spotted woodpecker, and I have occasionally observed with binoculars a small, sparrow-sized woodpecker, clinging to tree trunks, high in the tree canopy. Otters have also been seen in the park, but I have not been fortunate to see one, as yet.

Bute Park is a wonderful place, and a real gem in the heart of Cardiff. Please come and visit if you can. I know you will not be disappointed.

This article has been previously published in *Evergreen Magazine.*

WALKING THE WELSH JURASSIC COAST

It was a warm, sunny day in the middle of May. I began my walk on the Welsh Coastal Path on the cliffs at Penarth, in the direction of St Mary's Well Bay. It was a journey which would take me back, not only into history, but into prehistory itself. In the space of a few miles, I would encounter the building known as Marconi Tower, the abandoned ruins of Lavernock Fort, and an area on the beach where the fossilised skeleton of the first meat-eating dinosaur to be found in Wales was recently discovered.

The walk was clearly signposted, and although a thick tangle of hedgerow obscured the sea view and the precipitous cliffs, there were occasional gaps in the hedge where I could gaze out to sea. The path was pretty flat with only a few slight inclines to contend with, so walking wasn't at all difficult. Inland, arable fields stretched for some distance, whilst alongside the path delicate butterflies such as orange tips, speckled woods and green-veined whites flitted between wild flowers. In the spring sunshine, blackbirds and the occasional thrush sang melodiously from deep in the tangle of hawthorn, whilst in the blue skies above gulls wheeled and soared on the thermals.

At one point, the path dropped to beach level and rose again, and it was then that I came across a small and rather innocuous ivy-covered building on the clifftop, Marconi Tower. It was here in 1897 that the first wireless signals were exchanged between Lavernock Point and Flat Holm Island. Not far from the hut, and standing on the cliff edge, was a Royal Observation Corps observation post. During the war, volunteer ROC observers spotted many German planes approaching from across the channel, and activated air raid warnings in nearby Penarth. In early 1962, a nuclear bunker was completed at Lavernock Point for the ROC, with instruments to detect nuclear explosions, and warn the public of fall out, but this was closed and abandoned in 1975 after repeated break-ins by vandals. Marconi's transmitted messages were a momentous event in history, and a plaque inscribed in a perimeter wall of the nearby St Lawrence Church commemorates that moment. The first ever message transmitted in Morse code actually read, 'Are you ready' followed by 'Can you hear me'. The reply received was, 'Yes loud and clear'. The Morse code recording slip for this first message is now kept in the National Museum of Wales. St Lawrence Church itself, constructed mainly of limestone, is believed to date back to 1769, and although it rarely opens now, has a beautifully tended graveyard which is a haven for wildlife.

My walk then took a slight detour inland, where I found Marconi Holiday Park. At the back of the holiday park you will find Lavernock Nature Reserve, which is a delight to behold. The nature reserve contains a wide variety of habitats including Jurassic limestone grass and scrub. The reserve is an important location for migrating birds, and is also known for its hay meadows where orchids, cowslips and the scarce Adder's-tongue Fern can be seen in season. The elusive purple hairstreak butterfly can also be spotted from time to time at Oak Copse, which is north of Fort Road.

Shortly after passing the reserve I came across the abandoned ruins of Lavernock Fort. This site has a very long history dating back to the 1860s, when the Royal Commission built the gun battery to protect the channel approaches to Cardiff and Bristol's shipyards during the short-lived conflict between France and Britain that followed the French Revolution. Before 1895, a fourth cannon was added to the gun battery, and in 1903 all four guns were replaced by two rapid-fire six-inch ex-naval guns. In the Second World War a searchlight battery was added, giving protection to shipping convoys between Cardiff, Barry and Flat Holm Island. Nowadays, the main section of the gun battery has been listed as an ancient monument, which includes the gun emplacements, crew and officers' quarters, and rangefinder observation position.

I'd been walking for a couple of hours now, and as I approached St Mary's Well Bay, I decided to sit down on the grass to eat my lunch. It was a great place to take a break.

Below me, at the base of the cliffs, in the quiet swell, the waves washed lazily against the rocks.

It was mid-afternoon as I retraced my steps back along the coastal path in the direction of Penarth. As I clambered down to the beach at Lavernock, I wondered what secrets the beach might hold, for in March 2014, two brothers and keen fossil hunters came across the discovery of a lifetime: the fossilised skeleton of a completely new species of dinosaur. The bones turned out to belong to the first meat-eating dinosaur to be found in Wales and a cousin of tyrannosaurus rex. The fossilised dinosaur bones were approximately 200 million years old, and when the dinosaur was alive it lived at a time when the Welsh climate was akin to that of the Mediterranean, with warm and shallow seas. The dinosaur would have stood less than three foot tall, was carnivorous and warm-blooded, and was probably covered in feathery-down and quills along its back. It walked upright on two legs and had a long tail. The dinosaur apparently died when it was young, close to the shoreline, and was fossilised in marine sediment along with other small sea creatures.

As I climbed back onto the coastal path, and neared the end of my walk at Penarth, I reflected on what a great day I'd had. I would recommend the walk to anyone. Whether you are a fan of nature, history, or prehistory itself, the Welsh Jurassic Coast is a brilliant place to explore. The walk is not difficult. Try it for yourself. Who knows what you might discover?

SEA LAMPREY

The sun was shining on a warm June day in 2011. I had worked up a sweat, cycling some ten miles along the river Taff, part of the national cycle network which led north from the centre of Cardiff, ending some fifty-five miles later in the town of Brecon. The trail itself runs in close proximity to the river for a number of miles.

Despite having 'once ran black with coal dust' – a legacy of the dark days of the mining industry in Wales – the Taff was now a much cleaner river which had seen the return of otters, salmon and sea trout. Indeed, I regularly observed kingfishers, dippers and various coarse and game fish along the river, including barbel which had been introduced to the water some twenty years before, and which were now being caught to weights over sixteen pounds.

But today, my rather unremarkable cycle ride was suddenly to become quite special. I'd stopped for a rest by the bridge at Blackweir, a mile from the city centre, just at the point where the dock feeder stream flowed out of the Taff itself, and into the magnificent arboretum of Bute Park. As I looked down into the shallow, fast-flowing waters of the feeder stream, I was amazed to see a pair of sea lamprey spawning. Having seen pictures of these eel-like creatures before, I knew that they were, without doubt, sea lamprey. The male, which was approximately four feet long, was engrossed in a mating ritual with a female about half his size. A redd had been dug, and he was gripping relatively large stones with his bony, suckered mouth, then moving them some distance away from the depression in the gravel the couple's love dance had created. I marvelled at the colours of their mottled backs as the pair continued with their sinuous, sensual embrace.

I was transfixed. Here within a stone's throw of the city centre of Cardiff, I was witnessing the mating ritual of a fish that fossil evidence has shown predates the dinosaurs. A fish with no scales, gill covers, or bony skeleton; a fish that is now an endangered species, and protected by law. To my right, on the far bank of the river, were the sports grounds of Cooper's Field, where hundreds of students from the local universities had gathered. Many were enjoying barbecues as they frolicked and lounged in the hot summer sun, all apparently blissfully unaware of the prehistoric creatures just a short distance away.

But now, back to the feeder stream, and something about the incredible life cycle of the sea lamprey. The sea lamprey, or Petromyzon marinus, to give it its Latin name, is a parasitic fish, using its suction cup-like mouth to attach itself to a wide variety of other fish, rasping away flesh with its probing tongue and teeth. Anticoagulants in the lamprey's mouth prevent the victim's blood from clotting, and those victims often die from loss of blood, or infection. Young lampreys, or ammocoetes, lie buried in the soft, silty beds of river margins. They are blind and feed on tiny particles in the water. After several years as larvae, they metamorphose into adults and migrate to sea estuaries where they parasitise other fish, returning to spawn in spring or early summer, usually on the stony ground of gravel beds. The adults do not feed after spawning and die within a few days. And that latter stage in the sea lamprey's life cycle – the spawning stage – the final act of the courting couple, was the scene that enfolded before my very eyes.

I had taken some photographs and sent them to the Environment Agency, now renamed Natural Resources Wales. Although my photos weren't of brilliant quality, the Environment Agency were very pleased to hear from me, and confirmed my sightings as rare sea lamprey.

Some days later, I returned to the same spot, and in the margins of the dock feeder stream, anchored amongst some stones, I saw what appeared to be the decomposing remains of a fish. Much of the body had already been eaten, so it was difficult to tell precisely what species it might have been. Whether it was the remains of a sea lamprey or not, I was glad I had witnessed the spawning sequence of the living fish. Fish that were around before the dinosaurs.

In June 2015, on three separate occasions, I was again fortunate to spot some sea lamprey spawning in the dock feeder stream. Over the course of three days, I counted eleven fish in total. Once again I reported my sightings to Natural Resources Wales, who informed their records department. In the seventeen years I have been cycling along the Taff Trail, it was only the second year I have witnessed sea lamprey spawning. I counted myself very lucky that I had witnessed such a rare sight.

I look forward to future summers in the hope that once again, I will witness the mating ritual of these rather unusual and somewhat special fish.

This article was previously published in *The Countryman* magazine, and *Fallon's Angler*

SHELLFISH CURRY

A number of years ago – well, at least twenty-five – when I was a lot younger and considerably more innocent, I rented a room in a shared house in a town somewhere in the West Midlands. I shall keep the precise location of that town a secret, not because of the fact that I am the burglar in this fishy tale, but because I rather naively participated in the consumption of the proceeds of that burglary.

The house that I lived in was populated by various nefarious characters, many who liked a drink, and some who survived on a diet of rough cider (scrumpy) and whatever cheap food they could purchase with their dole money. To their minds, a few pints of scrumpy were almost a meal in themselves. In reality, the only real solid foods they ate were supermarket value beef burgers and sausages, and only when they were ravenously hungry – BSE was only in its infancy at the time, and I think it unlikely it would have affected them even if they'd caught it!

I would like to point out that I had no choice in the selection of my housemates. They just moved in and out at will, or were evicted by the landlord, as the need arose. I suppose I could have moved out myself, but the house was both convenient and close to where I worked, so temporarily, that was that.

One day, a new tenant moved in. I was told later that he was 'a very good burglar', apparently earning this title consisted of carrying out many burglaries and not often getting caught. In this story, I would like to stress that I am in no way condoning burglary, but at the time the following incident took place, I was in the dark as to the extent of such nocturnal habits, and so consuming the proceeds of one of his big jobs seemed a harmless act!

One night he arrived back from one his night-time forays with twenty packets of multi-coloured prawns, which he said he had 'liberated' from the chest freezer of the local Chinese restaurant. The prawns, with ten to a bag, retailed at five pounds per packet and came in every colour of the rainbow; ranging from deep purples to vermillion reds and garish greens. In total, he had over one hundred pounds' worth of exotic, oriental shellfish, which it was decided would make the basis of a delicious Chinese curry.

As our resident hunter-gatherer, we left him to do the cooking, boil some rice, add some vegetables and the curry paste. In a few hours the curry was cooked and I sat down in the kitchen to join the two alcoholics and the burglar to taste the curry.

Well, to put it mildly, the curry was so incredibly salty that I found it completely inedible. The curry tasted as if a whole salt cellar had been added to the mix, and it was so absurdly acrid that I could only manage a couple of mouthfuls. I tried not to gag, but made my excuses and left for my room as I had work the next morning. The two alcoholics, soused with cider, and the burglar, who'd now long since joined them on the scrumpy, continued to devour the curry with relish. Alcohol had clearly clouded their judgement and numbed what taste buds they had.

The following day, on my return from work, we had a visitor to the house. Not the police, as you might think, but an ex-jailbird and experienced fisherman. The house seemed to attract ex-cons for some reason; I never knew why. When I told him about the curry, and showed him the remaining prawns, still in their packets, he fell about laughing and simply couldn't stop! Now, it transpired that the 'very good burglar' had actually burgled the chest freezer of the shop next door to the Chinese restaurant, and not the chest freezer of the Chinese restaurant itself. So, the liberated goods that had been cooked and added to the curry were in fact cured and dyed prawns, removed from the premises of the local angling shop. The likes of which were apparently a great bait for salmon!

I had another shift that night, as I worked in a pub at the time, and so with my stomach surprisingly still intact, I left for the pub with a wry smile on my face. I had a tale to tell, but have kept that tale secret until this very day.

Neither I, nor the burglar, ever told our alcoholic housemates of the true origins of the multi-coloured prawns; since it was deemed that both alcoholics possessed the constitutions of an ox, we decided that nothing that they ate could really harm them. And, indeed, they finished off the curry with relish!

Soon after this, the jobs of the 'very good burglar' came to an end, and he was jailed for a number of years. Needless to say, I quickly moved out of the house, and on to bigger and better things (and I don't mean bank jobs); careful to avoid salty shellfish burglars, and the inedible contents of certain fishy freezers to this very day.

Below is a recipe for dyed and curing prawns. I'm not sure if this was the precise curing formula for our prawns! Great for catching salmon; not so good for making curries!

Basic curing formula for 453 g of prawns (or monster mash as I call it!):

2 l of purified water
700 g of fine sea salt
27 g of sodium nitrite
66 g of sodium sulfite (optional, but it is recommended to add a little)

55 g cup white sugar
1 tbsp sodium metabisulfite (optional)
1/2 tsp krill powder (optional)

This article was published in *Waterlog Magazine.*

CRICKET BALLS AND KEBABS

I had cycled many miles along the Taff Trail over the years, thousands of miles in fact. My longest ride being a very arduous fifty-five-mile trip from Merthyr Tydfil to Brecon and then back to Merthyr Tydfil in the same day. I burnt off nearly four thousand calories, climbed high into the Brecon Beacons, and lost half a stone in weight on that particular ride. I'm glad I did it, but the journey was not really one for the faint-hearted, and one I would not like to repeat on a regular basis. Not bad, I thought, for someone who'd had four knee operations and an operation on his right hip! Still, most of my cycling along the Taff Trail – a Sustrans cycle route which stretches from Cardiff to Brecon for a distance of over fifty miles – was usually only short journeys of ten miles or so. I was always looking for some animal, fish, bird or scene to observe with my binoculars, or photograph with my camera. Indeed, I had fished the River Taff sporadically over the years, and the dock feeder stream which flowed out of the river by the fish pass at Blackweir. I loved fishing and being by the river, and the water drew me back time and time again like a magnet. If I was not fishing, I was watching.

On one particularly balmy summer day in 2010, after a round trip of some ten miles or so, I found myself back in Cardiff and wheeling my mountain bike across the Millenium Bridge, which spans the river between the magnificent arboretum of Bute Park and Sophia Gardens. The hallowed turf of the Millenium Stadium – now called the Principality Stadium – is perhaps quarter of a mile downstream, and the Swalec Stadium, the recently rebuilt home of Glamorgan cricket, even closer. As I crossed the bridge and looked down into the river, facing upstream in the direction of Blackweir, there they were in the shallows: two of the biggest perch I had ever seen in my life! Fry leapt in all directions, as those two hog-backed leviathans eyed them with steely resolve. In fact, the perch, one of which was approximately a foot long, and the other perhaps an inch bigger, never made a move towards the panicking minnows. They remained motionless at an angle of forty-five degrees to the bank, in little more than two feet of water, which was gin clear. Perhaps the mere presence of these giant predators was enough to terrify the fry, and leaping clear of the water as a shoal was simply a natural reaction to the presence of these river monsters.

I could only begin to guess the weight of the two perch. But, I would hazard a guess that either might be over three pound in weight, whilst the larger of the fish could have been approaching four pound. It is always difficult to estimate the weights of fish unless you actually have them on the bank; but one thing was for certain, I didn't need my binoculars to observe them!

But now, I would like to move on, and look at other instances of monster fish I have seen, or known to have been caught in the small stretch of water close to the city centre.

In the summer of 2014, an eighteen-pound-one-ounce barbel was pulled from the river, and although this was caught further upstream, many very large barbel have been caught within sight of the Swalec Stadium. The eighteen-pound barbel was a magnificent fish, and a record for the Taff. It was a female and was 'spawned out', but a fish like that could easily be a contender to break the British record, should it pile on the pounds.

I have my own unique theory as to why the fish have grown so large, and it doesn't involve bacon grills, luncheon meat, halibut pellets, or any other 'natural bait' for barbel. My theory takes me back to a very famous cricket match, and watching England play Australia in the Ashes series of 2009.

Cricket match, I hear you say. Well, I shall explain. I was there, at the Swalec Stadium, with my mate Craig, amongst the sell-out crowd who witnessed a remarkable sporting event in that summer of 2009. The sun was shining and the ale was flowing when England's last wicket pair of Jimmy Anderson and Monty Panesar – yes, Monty who can't bat for toffee – clung on to thwart the Australians in a match that will go down in folklore as one of the most unlikely draws in test history! The crowd cheered every dot ball, and it felt like we had won the match. Cricket balls regularly ended up in the river as belligerent batsmen belted the leather off the cherry and out of the stadium, but when Monty smashed a six out of the ground and into the river, I was sure I must have been dreaming, or drunk!

And that, in essence, forms part of my theory as to why the fish in the river had grown so large. Yes, they were certainly eating bacon grills and luncheon meat, and probably vast quantities of halibut pellets as well; but occasionally, the very largest fish – particularly the barbel – were swallowing cricket balls whole, bulking up for the angler who just couldn't wait to catch that record fish! And if they weren't swallowing the occasional cricket ball, no doubt they were snacking on leftover pies and kebabs thrown into the river by worse for wear weekend revellers. Yes, the fish had grown fat on cricket balls, pies and kebabs, and thus had become true River Taff monsters!

But now, on a serious note folks, the eighteen-pound-one-ounce female barbel, caught some distance from the city centre, was really a magnificent fish, and shows the true potential of the water. And good luck to the angler who catches any fish approaching her weight!

This article was previously published in *Waterlog* magazine.

CORNISH TIME

The Housel Bay Hotel

Two Cornishmen on the coastal path of the Lizard Peninsula – examples of the local wildlife!

The gate to the most southerly house in Britain

The now defunct lifeboat station on the Lizard Peninsula

Kynance Cove

My bike, the faithful steed!

The ponds in the Lost Gardens of Heligan

IN MEMORY OF MARY GILLHAM

Image courtesy of SEWBReC's (South East Wales Biodiversity Records Centre) Dr Mary Gillham archive project, funded by the heritage lottery fund

Fox close to the Memorial Fields

The hide in the Memorial Fields

IN SEARCH OF EMPERORS

A male emperor moth

A female emperor moth, image courtesy of Derek Whiteley

Views of Howden Reservoir, the Peak District

The author in the Peak District

THE BEAUTY OF BUTE PARK

Various views of Bute Park

THE HIDDEN GEMS OF BARRY ISLAND

Jackson's Bay

Whitmore Beach

A rusting hulk in the old harbour

CRICKET BALLS AND KEBABS

Views of the River Taff, Cardiff

WALKING THE WELSH JURASSIC COAST

A view of the Jurassic Coastline

Saint Lawrence Church, Lavernock

Cemetery at Saint Lawrence Church, Lavernock

SHORT STORIES

A SEASONED OLD MOTH

The hawkmoth crawled across the window, his feathery antennae flickering against the glass. He was only small, insignificant to some, yet his desire for escape was overwhelming. Like many moths, he'd been trapped this way before; drawn through a gap in the window by the golden glow of the house lights. He always escaped. Lights fascinated him, drew him like a magnet. And, although there was danger in some, these particular beacons in the blackness had never threatened him. As he crawled higher, he felt the cool draft of perfumed air which meant freedom. When he beat his wings, blood flowed into his web-like veins, and he leapt from the window ledge.

The hawkmoth flew low over pines, skimming the treetops. Here he was safe from the fierce creatures which hunted the darkness. A bat had almost speared him with its razor-sharp teeth. He'd managed to escape, emitting piercing, squeaking sounds which had confused the bat's radar, before diving for the sanctity of the forests and a moss-covered tree trunk. He was lucky, the whole of his body and wings remained intact, and in a matter of hours he'd made a good recovery.

The hawkmoth was threatened by other creatures too. By night, cats, spider's webs and flashing car headlights had claimed many of his kin. He rarely flew by day; it was too dangerous, and although he possessed large, coloured eyes on his hindwings, which could frighten birds and other predators, he chose to rest in the trees until the sun went down.

He sensed the presence of the yellow moon, and white, pinpoint stars, high above him. Perhaps, rather surprisingly, these too had once been a threat. He'd tried to fly to these bright lights, spiraling into the endless black night like some winged angel, until overcome by exhaustion, he'd plummeted back to earth. It was the pine forest which had saved him once again, breaking his fall with its spongy canopy of leaves. Then there was the time when he'd flown close to the orange flames of a bonfire. Many before him, hypnotised by its warm glow, had plunged straight for the inferno's heart and been instantly vapourised. But then he was a seasoned old moth. He had learnt much about danger, and although now ravenous with hunger, he sensed the first rays of the morning sun. He would feed tomorrow. Now, he would seek out the sanctuary of a great green pine.

The following evening the hawkmoth again found himself drawn through a gap in a window. He'd fed on the sweet nectar of a forest rose which invigorated and enabled him to fly far. Strange scents came to him as he struggled for grip on the glass. Here it was warm; not the raging heat of a blazing bonfire, but a comforting warmth. It was the yellow light which first attracted him, the golden glow in the blackness which had drawn him through the open shop window. To his right, a new light flickered, and with the intoxicating nectar coursing through his veins, his judgement became clouded. As he flew towards it, its electric-blueness baffled, then fried his tiny brain.

'Glad you bought that flycatcher, eh Terry?'

'Yea, I hate damn moths! They get everywhere!' the shop owner grunted, as he wiped his nose on his shirtsleeve, before serving up more greasy chips.

By morning, the flycatcher was ready for emptying, and the hawkmoth just one more insect left glued to its grill.

Not far away, in a water meadow, close to the great pine forest, the first small caterpillars were emerging from their eggs. As sunlight glistened in the dewdrops of the morning, and the busying of buzzing insects filled the air, a female hawkmoth nestled against the trunk of a tree to rest.

This story was published in *The Countryman* magazine.

NO ORDINARY JOE

Joe Stevens loved secret places, and the caravan perched high on top of the cliffs, hidden in the ancient wooded glade, had become his sanctuary. Light pollution here was minimal, and at night he could watch meteors streak through luminous skies, dream of distant planets, and listen for the rustling and scuttling of the forest's creatures as they went about their business.

The cliffs rose vertically and majestically to a height of some two hundred metres. By day, gulls and ravens battled for supremacy and nesting rights in the skies above the tangled foliage which strangled the cliff face. A pair of peregrines: a young falcon and her mate, a tiercel of some experience, had constructed a nest made of skeletal sticks on a ledge which was now strewn with feathers and bones.

From a vantage point in the crown of an old oak tree, Joe had watched the pair through binoculars, marvelling at the female's unflinching patience, as she brooded her three chicks, whilst the sun beat down from a cloudless sky, and swarms of biting flies circled the nest, tormenting her. The haunting cries of the tiercel competed with those of the squabbling gulls and ravens as he stooped upon wood pigeon after wood pigeon to snuff out their lives. But it was night now, and Joe was tired and ready for sleep. He drifted into a dream-filled slumber, as a cool breeze wafted the night's scents through the trees.

Joe Stevens woke at first light, lit the wood stove inside his caravan, and enjoyed a breakfast of strong black coffee and an omelette made with oyster and chanterelle mushrooms, which he'd foraged in the woods. A warm September sun, some bright blue butterflies, and the melodious voice of a song thrush kept him company as he wound his way down the precipitous cliff path and into Jackson's Bay.

It wasn't long before he was casting his powerful beach-caster way out into the surf, in pursuit of anything edible he could catch. The big pollack took his crab bait almost instantly, and the line screamed as it was torn from his reel. Joe fought for almost half an hour to bring the heavy fish to the beach. He dispatched it, with some reluctance, and then lay the pollack, which appeared to glisten in the late summer sun, in a shallow rock pool to keep it fresh as the day warmed up. Gently, he bathed the body with seawater, as if anointing it; marvelling at the magnificence of the fish as it lay, as if in state, amongst the translucent prawns and brightly coloured anemones in the weed-strewn rock pool. He then rebaited his hook, and cast out again.

In spite of fishing until dusk, he caught nothing else that day, and as the sun dipped below the horizon and bats emerged from their roosts to trawl for insects, Joe Stevens carried his catch, as he had done so many times before, back to the top of the cliffs, and to the caravan which had become his spiritual home.

That night, as he lay in the wooded glade, staring deep into space and dreaming of distant planets, the northern lights, in all their glory, swirled hypnotically across pristine, unpolluted skies.

He slipped effortlessly into a deep sleep, whilst the sounds and scents of the ocean cleansed his soul.

This story was published in *Fallon's Angler.*

PIT PONIES

The old miner fished the flooded quarry on occasion. His mind was not what it used to be, but fishing relaxed him, and brought back memories of his youth when he was strong, fit and vigorous. He fished with light tackle, from an old wooden platform which jutted out from the weed-covered bank, for the flotillas of red-finned roach and rudd which patrolled the shallows of the cold, clear waters.

The quarry held many secrets; huge pike, like crocodiles, and great eels like miniature anacondas were rumoured to inhabit its dark and tangled depths. On the spartan cliffs which towered above its steeply wooded sides, ravens and peregrine falcons had constructed their stick-like nests. And amongst the reeds, in the hidden recesses of the mist-shrouded margins, the ghostly boom of a single bittern would often echo for miles across the secluded body of water.

The old miner felt a sharp tug on his line, and watched the tip of his vintage cane rod bow to the water's surface. He reeled in a beautiful, scale-perfect roach of about one pound, then quickly unhooked and released it, only to watch it vanish back into the depths from whence it came.

A pair of courting swans, their plumage as white as snow, drifted spectrally in and out of the mist which was now swirling across the pool. He felt a second sharp tug on his line and unhurriedly reeled in a tiny rudd, which weighed no more than a few ounces. He lovingly cradled the fish in one hand, admiring its unbridled beauty, before once again releasing it back into the icy depths. From somewhere in the woods, high above him, the haunting cry of a roosting tawny owl permeated the silence. The unearthly 'kee-wik! kee-wik!' of its call, brought him back to reality with a shudder.

The accident in the mine was more than fifty years ago, but the memories of the tragedy were still both vivid, and painful, for the old man. His thoughts meandered back to the days of his youth, and how he'd cared for and managed his beloved pit ponies. In the shaft mine the ponies were stabled underground; it was his responsibility to muck out and feed them on a diet of chopped hay and maize, and bring them to the surface for respite from their arduous and dangerous work beneath the earth. Typically, the ponies would work an eight-hour day, during which they could easily haul thirty tons of coal in coal tubs along the narrow-gauge railway. An average lifespan for a pony was no more than four years, so anything the old miner could do to prolong and improve the quality of his horses' lives, made him feel content.

A particular favourite of his had been the white stallion called Pegasus; the strongest and most sure-footed pony he had ever known. Pegasus had lived a long life hauling those heavy coal tubs in the bowels of the earth, but then the old miner had taken particular care of him, and had given him extra rations when he could. And Pegasus could eat! Oh, how that stallion could eat!

But those times were long gone, and Pegasus and all the other pit ponies had gone with them. And now, as dusk approached, the old miner was alone with his memories, and his vintage cane rod. His rod bowed once more to the water's surface, and once again he was cradling a beautiful, scale-perfect rudd of perhaps half a pound in the palm of his hand. He slipped it back into the pool, and it swam off into the ethereal depths.

Other creatures were about now; a dog fox barked from somewhere in the distance, and tiny bats swept the pool's surface for any small insect they could find. A sharp wind picked up, masking the tunnelling and scuttlings of the smaller creatures in the undergrowth.

The wind also masked the first footfalls of the larger animals. But he knew they'd come. They always did, once a year, on the anniversary of the explosion which had destroyed and flooded the mine. He could hear them now; the sound of their hooves clip-clopping on the paths which wound down through the woods, as they trotted through the trees.

The old miner put down his rod, put his hand into his pocket, and reached for the large, cubed sugar lumps which he knew they liked. Through the mists he moved imperceptibly towards them. It was the white stallion which nuzzled his chest first, then one pony after another did the same. He greeted them like long lost friends; he stroked them, offering each one a sugar lump, then ran his wiry fingers through their damp manes and along their powerful backs. He felt their cold breath on his face, and sensed the longing, knowing look in their dark eyes.

Time seemed to have no meaning now, and as the sky blackened, and a full moon emerged from behind its shield of freezing cloud, the old miner watched the pit ponies vanish like spectres into the trees. He followed, melting into the ether.

As the sun rose above the haunted pool, little moved, except the mists and the swan-spirits which swirled across the water's surface, and the shoals of red-finned roach and rudd which patrolled the margins of its icy depths.

SHE STOOPS TO CONQUER

The peregrine flew high over the city. Far below, myriad gulls soared and wheeled upon the thermals which shimmered in the heat of the summer skies. Born some distance to the south, two years before, on the storm-lashed cliffs of Southerndown, she had flown inland to seek a mate and raise a brood of young, on a ledge of the clock tower of city hall.

Her vision was acute; so acute in fact that she could see a student reading a book from a mile away. She paid little heed to the girl who was lounging lazily on the lawns in front of the civic buildings, but instead focused the dark pupils of her eyes on the pigeons resting amongst the stonework. Her mate, known as a tiercel, sat motionless on one of the stone cherubs, which jutted out from a ledge just below the clock face. The arms of the cherub were held aloft as if in supplication. Two of their young, a male and a female, hunkered down in the nest to avoid the biting flies and heat which tormented them. A third chick, another female, and the strongest of the three, used her claws and head to nudge the carcass of a woodcock along the ledge on which their nest of sticks was located. With her sharp beak, she picked at the scant remains of the carcass.

A few hundred feet below, powerful telescopes and binoculars were being trained on the nest from an RSPB marquee, staked out on the lush grass. Searching questions were being asked of one of their volunteers. 'Do they eat mice, and can I have one as a pet?' screeched an excited young girl of about ten years of age. The volunteer laughed, then explained that occasionally peregrines would take mice, but their main prey was actually pigeons, and that it was not appropriate to have one as a pet. At first, the girl seemed disappointed, but she soon perked up as the volunteer explained how the peregrines had come to nest in the city, then how they had chased some ravens from the clock tower, before commandeering the ravens' nest of sticks.

He continued to entrance the excitable school party with further gems about the birds, including the fact that the peregrine was the fastest bird in the world, and could fly at speeds up to two hundred miles per hour in a stoop as it dispatched its prey. All the children were eager to use the telescopes and binoculars in an effort to view the birds.

As the school party moved on, and into the museum, the volunteer sensed a new-found fascination amongst the children for the birds of prey. He hoped that fascination would last for the rest of their lives.

Far above all the commotion on the ground, the adult female began her arcing flight towards the heavens. As she gained height, moving effortlessly into the azure blue, the bronze hands of the clock struck midday. In the brilliant sunlight, some two miles above the marquee below, she folded back her slate grey wings, tucked in her legs, and began to stoop. The pigeon knew nothing as it was struck at two hundred miles per hour with a clenched foot like a steel mace, which broke its neck in an instant.

As the falcon swooped beneath her prey to grasp the dead bird in her claws, a single drop of bright red blood plummeted to earth, smearing the pages of a book which lay open in front of a student who lounged lazily on the lawns in front of the civic buildings. It was a book entitled She Stoops to Conquer, a play by the Irish writer, Oliver Goldsmith. It was the student's shrieks of alarm which startled the crowds, and not the screeching of the falcon, which carried the dead bird to the nest to be plucked. The shrill, eerie cries of her chicks cut through the oppressive summer heat like a knife. Systematically, the falcon's beak worked like scythe as she opened the flesh.

LADY OF THE LAKE

The lake shimmered in the oppressive heat. Clouds of midges swarmed in their millions, rising like a dark, billowing, blanket to the top of the brooding scree. The swallows had swept in many moons ago; crossing the vast sands of the Sahara Desert, flying over the sea and skirting the Atlas Mountains of Morocco before arriving at their summer feeding grounds. Their pilgrimage north had seen them nesting in the abandoned farmhouses and barns dotted about the edge of the lake. And now, as they darted amongst the clouds of midges, snapping up insects with their tiny beaks, they gorged themselves; for soon, like the midges, they would be gone.

In the cold, clear waters of the brook, the lady of the stream – a grayling of indeterminate age and over three pounds in weight – drifted nonchalantly in the rich, oxygenated water. Fry flashed about her, flickering silver and gold amongst the water crowfoot and across the shadows of the sun-drenched gravel. The grayling was carried by the current into the lake. As she rose to take a fly on the surface, she extended her large dorsal fin, and her mouth sucked in the tiny morsel. Languidly, she swam deeper, and the underwater landscape loomed large before her. A sunken rowing boat, part obscured by a turf-like meadow appeared in the distance, and tall, dense banks of weed rose from the lake bed, seeking the warming rays of the summer sun. Above her, lily pads cast dark shadows in the shallows, and shoals of bleak, roach and rudd meandered about the submerged forest, safe from predatory pike.

The grayling swam onwards and more familiar objects loomed into view. She swam towards the shelf, as she always did. She had known the reef on the shelf for many years. It had provided her with shelter and sanctuary when she was young, and now, it was a place which drew her like a magnet. Sunlight glinted on the surface, and her silver flanks flashed as she rolled.

The thing, bound with ropes and wrapped in a carpet, swayed in the current. From beneath the carpet, a large eel emerged, and then momentarily became entangled in the hair of the thing before returning to its lair. Lead piping, encased in concrete anchored the thing to the reef.

When divers found the wax-like figure, Susie Jones had been in the lake for 20 years. Some months later, her husband was apprehended, tried, and found guilty of her murder. He died in jail.

On the anniversary of her disappearance, anchored to the reef where the body of Susie Jones had been entombed for those twenty years, a small, marble cross was erected in her memory.

As the lady of the stream swam towards the shelf, the new thing in the shape of a cross loomed into view. She swam amongst the strands of weed, tangled like human hair, which clung to the marble.

The swallows would return soon; the lake would once again shimmer in the oppressive heat, and clouds of midges would once more swarm in their millions rising like a dark, billowing blanket to the top of the brooding scree.

THE MISTRESS OF THE WRECK

The great eel swam sinuously through the shattered wreck of the warship. She was over twenty years old, having being born a year before the sinking of the corvette, which had been split in two by a mine during the war, and then settled on its starboard side on the seabed.

Both fishermen and divers knew the giant eel well, for she'd been hooked and lost on many occasions, and, indeed, divers used to feed her on fish scraps until she became too large and intimidating for them to risk placing their hands before her cavernous mouth. The great eel could swim backwards too, and now, as she snaked tail-first inside the rusting, barnacle-encrusted funnel which had become her lair, she could sense a change in the currents which swirled sporadically around the wreck. A powerful storm was brewing; and it was time even for one as muscular as her to seek sanctuary inside the ship.

The crew of the Boa Pescador, were wise to remain in port, and ride out the storm which whipped white horses against her hull. Beyond the breakwater, the Atlantic Ocean raged in the darkness. Lying in his bunk, skipper Steve Barrett tossed and turned as the rains hammered like nails against the deck above his head. In the bunk opposite, his deck hand, Smiler, a veteran of many legendary conger fishing trips, lit a cigarette and watched the blue smoke drift imperceptibly towards the ceiling. A faint orange glow emanated from the single light bulb which flickered intermittently, casting dark, eerie shadows about the cabin. With the storm forecast to last until first light the fishermen waited with nervous anticipation for the winds to subside.

As dawn approached, the crew of the Boa Pescador began to stir in their bunks. Some four hours later, with the sea much calmer, and only a slight swell, the forty-foot trawler was steaming south-east in the direction of the battle-scarred fishing grounds.

With the baits cast, the Boa Pescador drifted almost silently over the wreck. Hundreds of feet below the mackerel flappers and whole pouting baits dangled enticingly only feet above the lair of the great eel. Shoals of smaller fish drifted in and out of the sanctuary of the wreck. Cod, pollack and haddock – creatures which the giant eel preyed upon – meandered between the strands of weed which covered the sunken warship like dead men's fingers. Brittle stars, spider crabs and one of the corvette's resident lobsters, moved at their own undetectable pace across the debris field which stretched for a quarter of a mile over the seabed.

Steve and Smiler waited eagerly for that first familiar tug on their lines. With the onset of dusk they knew their chances of catching a big eel increased. As darkness fell, the slight swell which had caressed the hull of the trawler for most of the afternoon, diminished until it was nothing. The Boa Pescador became becalmed in a glassy sea which seemed to stretch over the horizon and into infinity. Ten miles astern of the fishing boat the lights of Scarepoint Lighthouse flickered intermittently in the pale moonlight. A small ling was the first fish to be dragged from the depths, followed by a diminutive codling, and a pollack weighing about five pounds. Each fish was quickly dispatched by a sharp blow from a heavy priest.

An eerie calm which had engulfed the fishing boat was unexpectedly exacerbated by an icy mist which rolled in from somewhere far out in the Atlantic. The freezing mist swept across the boat's deck, enveloping the crew in a shroud as white as snow.

Hundreds of feet below, in the inky-blackness of her lair, the Mistress of the Wreck had smelt the bait. The great eel stirred, then loosened her grip on the twisted metal inside the corvette's funnel. She swam out into open water to inspect the offerings which now dangled enticingly only feet from her enormous head. Cautiously, she circled the fish baits; examining them first from above, and then below, with her sensitive mouth. The powerful currents jolted the bait upwards in a sudden, violent movement. Overcome by instinct the great eel clamped her enormous jaws around the whole pouting, and the vicious, steel hook bit deep into her flesh.

On board the Boa Pescador, Steve watched the powerful rod bend almost in half. Line zipped from his reel as the great eel began to turn and twist her body, simultaneously thrashing her massive head to and fro, in an effort to free herself from the cruel hook which had stabbed the inside of her mouth. Smiler grabbed Steve from behind, and clung to him like a limpet, to stop him from being dragged overboard. Five hundred feet below, in the dark depths of the Atlantic Ocean, the great eel was already backing into the barnacle-encrusted funnel that was her lair. But the tackle on board the Boa Pescador was strong. In fact, it was the strongest and most robust fishing tackle ever brought to these particular fishing grounds. Skipper Steve was determined, whatever the cost, to bring the monster eel on board his vessel, having enthusiastically sharpened the point of his six-foot-long gaff until he felt it could penetrate sheet metal.

In the icy depths of the Atlantic, the eel's body was now almost entirely inside the funnel; but the violence of her struggles had only forced the vicious hook deeper into the flesh of her mouth. There was no way she could dislodge it, and severing the wire trace attached to the hook was proving impossible.

Slowly, the skipper on board began to gain ground on the giant fish. Inch by inch the eel was pulled from her sanctuary and dragged across the rough, rocky ground of the debris field, before being yanked unceremoniously towards the surface of the ocean. In desperation, she continued to thrash her head and twist her enormous body, in a futile attempt to break the line. She could not smash this fishing tackle as she'd always done in the past, and now she was being dragged ever closer to the ocean's surface, where Smiler, who still had hold of his skipper in a tight embrace, waited with eager anticipation to impale her with the needle-sharp gaff.

After a fight lasting more than an hour, the giant eel's head broke the ocean's surface for the first time, only feet from the hull of the fishing boat. She twisted her body in one final, violent movement, before flopping limply in what was now a gentle swell.

With sweat pouring from his brow, the trawler's skipper reeled in his line and brought the great eel closer to his boat. Alongside him, Smiler, who had by now released his grip on his captain, waited with the gaff to impale the eel's flesh, then haul her from the water. Momentarily, both men stared in utter disbelief at the sheer size of their exhausted quarry. Then, just as the stricken creature was no more than a foot from the boat, the eerie grip of the mist which swirled across the deck seemed to intensify. Wisps of a new kind of mist appeared as if from nowhere; some rising from the very depths themselves, from a place so dark that it was incomprehensible to the crew of the Boa Pescador.

The fishermen could only look on in horror, as at first, those mists began to take on the form of a human arm, and then a human hand; a vaporous, skeletal hand with defined fingers and a thumb, which were whiter than snow. As the bony fingers of the hand reached forward to snap the wire trace which held the great eel, Smiler toppled backwards onto the wooden deck, hitting his head and knocking himself unconscious. The sharpened point of the gaff landed only inches from his face. In a whirlpool of water the great eel was sucked back into the depths.

In his cabin below deck, Smiler sat shivering and babbling uncontrollably, an ice pack pressed to the enormous bruise on his head. In the wheelhouse, Steve gunned the trawler's engine to its maximum, his face ashen, a haunted, terrified look in his eyes.

He knew he'd just seen a ghost.

In time, the wreck of the war grave became quiet, and the sanctuary of the great eel was once again undisturbed. On the ocean's surface, ten miles from the battle-scarred fishing grounds, the lights of Scarepoint Lighthouse flickered intermittently in the mists which held them in a vice-like grip.

This story was published in *Waterlog Magazine.*

THE SPECIMEN HUNTER

The specimen hunter arrived at the old fisherman's cottage just as the light was fading, and the pipistrelle bats, which roosted in the dusty attic, began their nightly trawl for insects.

The cottage was redolent with age, and icons of fishing memorabilia, including stuffed pike and salmon weighing almost forty pounds, covered the walls. It was difficult to make out the names of those anglers on the faded brass plaques who'd caught the fish, but the young man guessed that some of the specimens, judging by their worn condition, must have been caught in the nineteenth century when Queen Victoria sat on the throne. He marvelled at the greenheart rods, horsehair lines, and enormous flies – the latter made from the feathers of rare and exotic birds – standing proud and erect in one corner of the room.

On the mantelpiece, above the hearth, he noticed the empty vase, so beautifully and intricately painted with an image of a man in top hat and tails, hooking a salmon on a fast-flowing river. Then he remembered. Damn! He'd forgotten the flowers! The landlady was adamant that he must purchase flowers to put in the vase, no doubt to perfume the room, which had an overpowering damp and musty smell that seemed to permeate the very walls themselves. But the young man's mind was on fish, and that specimen wild brown trout he intended to catch tomorrow. The flowers could wait. He'd pick some up later. Fishing, an obsession for the specimen hunter, could not.

He carried his bags to the bedroom, unpacked and took a quick shower. Then, overcome by a sudden sense of creeping fatigue – he blamed it on the long drive from the city – slid seamlessly beneath the crisp sheets on the four-poster bed. Outside, the night came alive. A tawny owl hooted from the treetops of an ancient oak, and roe deer foraged in the mists which swirled at edge of the forest. The sounds of badgers snuffling and shuffling in the garden in their endless search for earthworms did nothing to disturb him. And even the cries of an old fox, barking from its secret haunt in the depths of the forest, did not interrupt his dreams of fish. The specimen hunter slept soundly throughout the night.

He rose early the next morning, cooked a light breakfast of two fried eggs and some toast, then made his way along an overgrown twisting path in the direction of the river, which was hidden deep in a valley some half a mile from the cottage.

On the river, the young man cast a black gnat to the brown trout sunning themselves between the strands of water crowfoot. With his polaroids he could see that there were some real specimens in this river, perhaps fish of over five pounds, but they were proving impossible to catch. He changed flies, moved stealthily from location to location, but with conditions against him as the summer sun beat down from a cloudless sky, he simply could not tempt a fish to take his fly. He left the river in early evening, angry with himself that he did not catch. He would be back the next day to try again.

As he crossed the threshold of the cottage, the damp and musty smell which had been overpowering on his arrival the previous day, now almost choked him. Briefly, he gagged, then remembered the flowers and the owner's strict instructions that he should buy some roses to place in the vase above the hearth. He attempted to chuckle. Perhaps there was method in her madness, after all! But, he quickly dismissed those thoughts of flowers. The young man could put up with the smell and the damp; after all, he had fish to catch, and a specimen brown trout at that. He would have to rethink his tactics for the next day.

The cottage came alive at night. A full moon hung above the restless forest which moved with the scuttling and rustlings of the creatures of the dark. An icy mist seemed to grip the very walls themselves, as finger-like tendrils scratched, then permeated the very stonework. The young man slept, oblivious to the dank and odious presence which had entered his room. As that presence crept higher up the bed, he was suffocated, barely moving as the last breath was squeezed from his body. A bouquet of dead roses was placed next to his corpse.

The landlady, an old hag of indeterminate age, kept them in large glass cases in her cellar. The young man, strong and muscular as he was, would make a fine addition to her collection, and in the next few days she would prepare, then stuff him in a fly fishing pose. In the cellar, which appeared to have no entrance or exit, and which seemed to stretch to infinity and beyond, her collection was growing. There was a coracle fisherman from Wales, netting some sewin; and an Edwardian lord, smoking a pipe, complete with ghillie, hooking a mahseer from a raging torrent somewhere in India. And, of course, there was that very fine old Victorian gentleman; her first love, casting for salmon on a fast-flowing river in top hat and tails, a red rose gripped tightly between his polished teeth.

The old hag; a legendary water-witch, cackled from somewhere deep in the darkest corner of the forest.

'They always forgot the flowers!'

And, of course; she could never forgive them for that.

A TALE OF TWO RIVERBANKS

Close to where a line of verdant willows wept shade into the river, the old ferryman observed the otter cub leave the main watercourse, then swim up the stream. As the cub dived, he watched the trail of bubbles burst upon the surface, marking the progress of the submerged creature in the direction of its holt.

As he stood on the riverbank, the cold air of an autumn morning made him tighten the woollen scarf around his neck. As the mists swirled about him, he glimpsed the sleek form of the otter cub leave the water, then vanish deep beneath the roots of an ancient oak.

Somewhere, not too distant from the jetty on which he now sat, the familiar cries of a roosting tawny owl permeated the silence.

The first customers for the ferry were yet to appear. He reached into his haversack, taking out a flask of hot steaming tea. In spite of the cold, the old ferryman loved these misty mornings. They were so peaceful and uplifting. And as he sipped on the sweet, dark liquid which slipped down his throat like nectar, a kingfisher, bright as a blue spear, darted in front of him. When he'd finished his tea, he began his daily walk upstream where he'd place flowers on his wife's grave in the ancient chapel grounds.

He walked leisurely; in spite of his age, his legs were strong, the years of working his punt and an active rural lifestyle maintaining the strength in his wiry physique. He listened for the sounds of the river as water tumbled over the weir. When he approached the waterfall, a silver salmon leapt, then twisted in the air. Air was not the salmon's natural element, but it appeared that the fish was actually leaping for joy, and for an instant, was briefly at home in the cold autumn light. As it flopped back into the river to hide in a deep pool, it startled a pair of dippers who flew out from where they'd been nesting behind the curtain of spray. The old man marvelled at these little birds, how they too could bestride both elements of air and water, just like the salmon. He loved to watch them and their white bibs as they bobbed up and down on a favourite rock, before diving at the water's edge to feed on the small creatures which lived close to the riverbank.

As he approached the ancient chapel, up a twisting and winding path some distance above the river, the mists which had accompanied him along the valley began to vanish. When he entered the graveyard, he reached inside his haversack for the small bunch of flowers he always picked from his garden to place on his wife's grave. A great sadness overcame him as he placed the red and yellow flowers against the headstone. Looking about him, he admired the other graves; each meticulously tended, each adorned with fresh-cut blooms. In summer, he'd spend more time in the graveyard; soaking up the sunshine, watching the garish butterflies flit along the hedgerow and amongst the wild flowers which grew in untouched profusion around those headstones. In autumn, and as the winter storms approached, he spent less and less time in the hallowed chapel grounds.

After what seemed an age, he left the churchyard behind, then slowly headed back in the direction of the towpath. Time passed quickly for the old ferryman, and lost in reverie as he was, early morning had merged into late afternoon before he knew it. As he arrived back at the jetty, the sun was already sinking below the horizon.

Swirling mists had enveloped the first of the ferry's passengers in a shroud as white as snow. A pale, yellow moon hung in the darkening sky.

'Good evening Mr Thomas.'

'Good evening Ma'am! How are you and your husband, and the children?'

'Very well, Mr Thomas; very well!'

'Aah, and I see you've brought Shadow with you tonight. I assume he will be with you for the crossing?'

'Well, of course, Mr Thomas; what did you expect?'

The old ferryman did not reply, but a polite nod and a warm smile of recognition passed fleetingly between them. The family's pale complexions appeared to merge with the mists as they boarded the punt. Their dog Shadow, a moth-eaten, almost skeletal, but wily old sheepdog, was last to alight. The crossing was made in good, if quiet humour; the river calm. As the punt nudged the far riverbank and its adjoining jetty, the family of four prepared to disembark.

'I presume there will be no charge tonight, Mr Thomas?'

'No, Mrs Jones. Is there ever?'

No one spoke again, and as the old ferryman watched the four figures disappear into the mists in the direction of the ruined village, with their skeletal dog close at heel, he pushed his punt out into deeper water.

In a garden adjacent to one of the ruined cottages, Mrs Jones straightened up the small cross, which was weather-beaten and leaning to one side. She brushed the wet cobwebs from the rotten old wood, then read aloud the inscription carved into its gnarled grain:

'IN MEMORY OF ALL THOSE WHO DIED IN THE GREAT FLOOD OF 1836'

Emily and James, their two young children, and their ragged dog, Shadow, had long since vanished into the woods to frolic amongst the trees.

The couple held hands as they walked amongst the ruins.

As the old ferryman approached the far riverbank, a second family was waiting on the jetty, eager to make the crossing. They, too, had pale complexions like the mists.

From somewhere in the darkness, came the familiar call of a roosting tawny owl. The silhouette of an otter cub left its holt, then swam up the stream.

The night was peaceful; the river calm.

The old ferryman, at one with the burgeoning silence.

This story was published in a book, *Willow Pitch 2*, from Little Egret Press.

THE BOILIE

Terry Smith liked to hang around the bushes. Camouflaged to the hilt with ex-military fatigues, and with his face painted, he blended in with the undergrowth like one of his many movie idols. Stalking carp was his life, and catching Goliath had become an obsession. The legendary carp – a fish hardly ever seen, but reputed to have grown to a mythical, almost monstrous size – had allegedly been brought to the lake from France in the back of a transit van some years before.

A British record was on, and Terry Smith wanted that record.

As he looked out across the great expanse of water, he flicked a lever on his handheld controls, and watched The Boilie's conning tower slip below the surface. Based upon the specifications of the most advanced German U-boat of World War Two, the miniature submarine was no more than a metre long, and was armed with a camera to spot fish and other targets. It carried a variety of baits within its torpedo tubes, and had been customised in absolute secrecy in his lock-up in Essex.

No one knew of the existence of The Boilie, and when other anglers' bait boats such as The Dirty Sue, Lady Godiva and Madonna, mysteriously vanished into the weedy depths whilst on clandestine bait dropping missions, it was blamed on the powerful underwater currents and whirlpools which swirled beneath the lake's surface. Even when the ducks, coots and moorhens began to disappear, it was blamed on pike. No one had an inkling that it was the work of Terry Smith and The Boilie, as the unfortunate birds were torpedoed with oversized halibut pellets containing small explosive charges, before being dispatched to a watery grave. Most of the other anglers had long since left the lake, believing the mythical carp Goliath uncatchable, and disillusioned by the loss of their beloved bait boats.

As dusk approached, Terry Smith emerged from the woods, then settled into his pitch. He brought The Boilie up from the lake bottom, and let the sub wallow in the shallows. With the light rapidly fading, he checked his bite alarms on his six rods, then disappeared into his bivvy for a brew and some scoff. He lay down his on bunk, before drifting into a fitful sleep.

The lake came alive at night, and a cool breeze wafted tendrils of mist across the water's surface. Nearby, crickets chirped in the long grass, and bats trawled the fading light in search of insects. From a hidden place, not far from its earth, a dog fox barked, and from high in an ancient oak tree a roosting owl called hauntingly to its mate.

Beneath the full moon, myriad fish rose to take flies on the water's surface, and the drowsy perfume of summer flowers filled the night air.

In his bivvy, Terry Smith had now fallen into a deep, almost drunken sleep; his senses subsumed to the intoxicating scent of those sweet summer flowers. So deep was his sleep, that he was oblivious to the movement in the undergrowth just outside his tent. It was the tendrils of bindweed that first wrapped around his ankles, then the stems of sweet scented Himalayan balsam. As the brambles sank their thorns into his thighs, it was far too late for Terry Smith.

On the lake, there was no one to hear him scream.

As his bivvy, rods and miniature submarine were being dragged beneath the water's surface, Terry Smith was already wedged deep beneath a rock on the lake bed; his body wrapped in a cocoon of waterweed, his mouth stuffed with nettles and biting stonecrop.

In time, other anglers returned to the lake with their reincarnated bait boats: Madonna, Lady Godiva, and The Dirty Sue 2.

And so, in time, did the ducks, coots and moorhens.

No trace of Terry Smith was ever found, and, perhaps for the best, Goliath was never caught.

Yet, legend has it, that on certain nights of the year, when the moon is full, and a dog fox barks from somewhere deep in the secret forest, that if you listen very carefully, you can just about make out the words: 'EL TEL'S SCORED!' and 'GET IN THERE BIG BOY!' emanating from somewhere deep beneath the cold, dark waters of the lake, before that cry is strangled, drowned, and then dissipated on the breeze.

But then maybe that's just a load of old tosh! Very much like this tale!

THE UNDEAD

The great barracuda hovered in the current above Paradise Reef. Nearby, bonefish flashed like jewels across the sand-flats. The reef teemed with all manner of life, and as the summer sun warmed the tranquil shallows of the lagoon, in the sandy spaces where the coral was less dense, garden eels swayed like dancers in the quiet current, darting as one into the sanctuary of their burrows at the movement of any shadow.

In the lush, mist-shrouded forests which meandered the length of the coastline, towering above the beach and ancient cliffs, parrots squawked, monkeys chattered, and gaudy, gossamer-winged butterflies sipped nectar from exotic flowers.

The canoes drifted in the slight swell. The current had carried the fisherman beyond the river mouth and past the quicksands which had swallowed up many of their ancestors. In the mangrove forests, where brackish water rose and fell with the tides, a unique community of plants and animals thrived in the pristine habitat. Populations of mudskippers and small crabs made the tangle of tree roots their home; the tiny fish seeking to outwit the sharp claws of the larger crabs by leaping for their lives as soon as danger threatened.

As the sun beat down from a cloudless sky, a shoal of flying fish launched themselves from beneath the hollowed-out hulls of the canoes. A pod of dolphins followed the shoal, and behind the dolphins came the larger predators. As the fishermen approached the great seamount, the slight swell dissipated and their canoes became becalmed. They baited their handlines with fish scraps before casting their hooks into the endless, hypnotic blue.

Far, far away, the first rumbles of simmering discontent echoed from deep inside the Smokey Mountains.

Some distance inside the National Park, the fishing fleet, headed by their flagship Typhoon, had set their long lines. The sharks they caught had their tails and fins sliced off, without a thought. Mutilated and bloodied, they were tossed back into the ocean to die in agony. The by-catch of drowned turtles and seabirds – some on the critically endangered list – were also tossed back into the ocean; just more flotsam and jetsam to be carried who knows where by the vagaries of the prevailing wind and currents.

In the lagoon, close to this shoreline, fishing with dynamite had long since destroyed the reef, and virtually all of its inhabitants. Here, there were no garden eels, and no bonefish flashed like jewels across the sand flats. And the last of the great barracuda had been blown from the water many years before.

High above what remained of the beach on these ancient cliffs, the once lush, mist-shrouded forests were just a far distant memory, and the iridescent parrots, chattering monkeys, and gaudy, gossamer-winged butterflies which used to sip nectar from exotic flowers, long since extinct. In their place stood a raft of cheap, foetid hotels and sleazy boarding houses; shrouded in the fog of pollution, and populated by the dregs of humanity.

Far out at sea, some three thousand kilometres from where the fishing fleet had set their long lines, the ocean floor erupted, rising and falling with unbridled violence as the great tectonic plates deep within the bowels of the earth collided. The earthquake registered a massive ten on the Richter scale, then the wave, small at first, gathered pace and height as it hurtled towards the coast. When the tsunami struck the fishing fleet, obliterating it in an instant, it was over twenty metres high. When it struck the coast, it was tall enough to smash into the raft of cheap hotels and sleazy boarding houses, splintering them into matchwood.

A week later, when the few survivors gathered on the ancient clifftop, moving amongst the squalor, stench of dead bodies and wreckage of their homes, they had the look of zombies about them. In time, the reef would become the paradise it once was, the undead would leave the coastline forever, and the lush, mist-shrouded forest would return in pockets to populate the ancient cliffs.

Three thousand kilometres to the south, untouched by any giant wave, the hunter-gatherers beached their canoes inside the sanctuary of the lagoon. They carried their small catch of snapper and grouper up the beach to their families in woven baskets. Their children laughed and frolicked on the pristine sands, and their womenfolk smiled; the broadest and deepest of smiles, greeting the fishermen with garlands of fragrant flowers like returning heroes.

In the lagoon, in the soft, sweet-scented moonlight, the great barracuda barely moved in the tranquil current which washed over the reef.

The forest awoke to a new world.

The sand flats were perfect in their silence; and the garden eels slept soundly in their burrows.

THE BOY AND THE BROOK

The construction of the waterwheel had breathed new life into the brook. The rotation of the wheel carried rich, oxygenated water from the waterfall which tumbled into the headrace. Some distance below the wheel, beyond the spume, the brook flowed more languidly, and in the quiet, deep holes beneath the entanglement of tree roots, the juvenile fish sought sanctuary. Minnows flashed silver in the sunlight, and from a perch high in the branches of a weeping willow, a bejewelled kingfisher waited to spear them.

On the banks, the sweet scent of dog roses perfumed the air, and nectaring bees, heavy and drowsy with pollen, flitted from flower to flower. Dragonflies hawked the length of the brook, snatching small insects on the wing, and at dusk, on occasion, an otter hunted for eels amongst the stones and secret places.

The small boy moved through the undergrowth like a veteran jungle warrior. He stooped low, moving silently, hardly daring to breathe. He held the old fly rod above his head, attempting to avoid the nettles and brambles which seemed intent on stinging, stabbing and lacerating his soft skin. In the deep pool, no more than a few feet in front of him, the jack pike loomed like a leviathan. The small boy marvelled at its colours; the shimmering green and golds of its skin, and the angular alligator head fixed with vicious, backward-facing teeth, waiting to impale any poor creature which passed too close to its jaws.

He was now almost clear of the undergrowth. The pike hung motionless before the weed in the dappled sunlight, and the boy tensed with anticipation. Then, ever so carefully, he drew himself up to his full height, pulled some line off the reel, raised the old cane rod above his head and with a few deft flicks of his wrist, cast his fly before the monster.

The fly landed with a small splash, a foot in front of the pike's head. With his free hand, and in a figure of eight, he began to retrieve the line. The pike remained motionless, showing no interest in the fly as it passed in front of its great snout, then beyond its mottled body. The small boy cast again; this time a side cast, flicking his line expertly before the beast. The pike leapt from the water and took the fly! It was tail walking! The small boy did not panic, but let the fish run to the white water just below the waterwheel. It shot up through the spume, tail walking once again, before being swallowed up by the torrent.

From its secret place, hidden amongst the tree roots, the otter slipped into the water, moving like a sinuous torpedo towards the pike. In the deep pool below the waterwheel, the otter bit the fish in half. For some time, the small boy watched the otter devouring his prize catch on the bank. He did not begrudge the otter its meal, and when he reeled in what remained of the pike's head, he harboured no resentment towards the creature.

As dusk fell, and the dark shapes of bats emerged from their roosts to trawl for insects, he left for home, and the comfort of a blazing log fire.

The old man struggled through the undergrowth as best he could. He found bending difficult now, and he no longer moved with the suppleness of youth. Breathing heavily, and with trembling hands, he held the battered old binoculars to his eyes. From behind a tree, he watched the otter family slip into the water. He smiled; a wily old smile, which in spite of his afflictions, showed he was at peace. The waterwheel still turned on its axis, just as it had done when he was ten, but now, like him, its movements were much slower, and considerably more laboured.

As the sun slipped lower on the horizon, and a jack pike – no longer the leviathan of his youth – drifted silently before the water crowfoot, he limped home to his slippers, fond memories, and the comfort of a blazing log fire.

A BREED APART

Where the land ended and the sea began was often a mystery. Each of the great rivers which emptied into the bay had deposited untold centuries of alluvial soil on the sandy and peaty shore. They created vast areas of marshlands, which, without perception, had become one with sea. The marshes, still impenetrable in many places and punctuated by tiny islands and pockets of forest, were the landscape of legends; and the souls who dwelt therein, a people apart. The marsh-men kept to themselves, and outsiders, unless they became lost, remained on the periphery of this isolated environment.

Today, one of the few eel-men who still fished the flooded channels, eased his punt through the floating mists, as dawn broke on an icy winter morning. In the reeds, a secretive water rail called to its mate, and a bittern boomed in the distance. As the sky lightened, and the mists dissipated, the eel-man moved closer to his traps. He moored his punt to an ancient wooden post at the side of the channel, then pulled his wicker baskets from the water. The eels were small; no more than a foot long, not like the ones he'd caught as a child when he'd fished with Old Tom. Eels then were long and fat, and often the length of a man's leg.

These eels were small and skinny and would not sell well at market. He emptied his meagre catch into a bucket at the bottom of his punt, then rebaited the baskets with strips of rabbit and shrimp, before lowering them back into the flooded channel. As he moved along the channel, trap after trap came up the same: devoid of any eel of any size, and half were completely empty. The children would go hungry once again.

The ramshackle cottage stood out like a beacon on the wooded island amongst the floating mists. The peat walls and thatched roof had been the home to eel-men for generations. The eel-man warmed himself in front of an open fire, where cut turf and the occasional log burnt brightly in the hearth, preventing tentacles of ice from spreading insidiously throughout the whole of the cottage. With the children away at their uncles in a distant part of the marsh, where the fishing was only marginally better, the eel-man ate what little food he had. A couple of small eels, which he'd smoked the previous year, and a small piece of stale, unleavened bread made up his supper.

He wrapped himself in a thick woollen blanket, and rocked himself to sleep in his chair.

Beneath the full moon, the spirit of the marsh was taking shape. In the flooded channel, a will-o'-the-wisp began to take on a human form. Glowing fire-red and holding a burning torch aloft, the figure, formed from the gases in the marsh, seemed to rise from the very depths themselves.

The fairy-fire moved with the tide, and with that tide came the great fish.

That night, as the old the eel-man slipped into a deep sleep, warmed before a blazing hearth, his dreams of a full belly would become a reality.

And the fairy-fire, the spirit of Old Tom, well, it was not seen again for a generation.

But the big eels were back, and they kept on coming; they sold well at market, and the children never went hungry again. And the landscape, as ever, remained a place of legends. And the souls who dwelt therein, always a breed apart.

THE GARDEN'S SECRETS

Hidden in the old tree stump, where the cat scratched and sniffed, below where the ivy crept along the wall, and behind the tangle of holly and brambles, the dormouse slept.

The old house, now just a ruin, was almost concealed by the mists which had risen from the cool waters of the lake; mists which now swirled and billowed into every crack and crevice of the crumbling structure. In the deepest parts of the lake, beside the great dam, the descendants of the wild carp, introduced to the tranquil waters by the monks centuries before, had grown huge in their pristine isolation. As the spring sun rose above the horizon and warmed the surface of the water, the mists faded and the first dragonflies and damselflies took to the wing.

In the walled garden, a stoat, still partly clothed in its winter coat, moved sinuously amongst the broken stones at the base of the wall. Her kits, well hidden behind a pile of old logs and moss, huddled together for warmth whilst their mother hunted for rats and rabbits in the undergrowth. Songbirds bathed in the lichen-encrusted fountains; fountains which had long ceased functioning, but whose weathered cherubs held up their arms in supplication, as if seeking salvation from the skies above. The trees swayed in the light breeze, and as the sun rose higher in those clear, azure blue skies, butterflies with orange-tipped wings swept the corridors of the secret maze. The garden was at peace; and still the dormouse slept.

By late afternoon, the wild carp, as if drawn by some invisible, inexorable force, left the seclusion of their weed-strewn isolation, and swam up the water column. As dusk inched ever closer to darkness, the mists rose once again from the water's surface, enveloping the old house in a white, billowing shawl which penetrated every crack and crevice. A lone, hooded figure drifted in and out of those mists as they swirled at the edge of the lake. He moved, as he'd done for generations now, almost without perception to an anointed spot at the top of the great dam.

As night descended like a black curtain, the first of the great fishes' mouths broke the water's surface. In the hypnotic moonlight, their huge, ghost-white shapes lit up the surface of the lake like creatures from ancient mythology. The hooded figure, so pale beneath his habit, broke and tossed leavened bread to them as he'd done now for so many years.

In the distance, badgers emerged from their sett, and a long-eared owl swept silently through the trees. Along the wall where the ivy crept, a ragged old tomcat of some great, yet indeterminable age, dropped to his familiar scratching post in the tangle of holly and brambles at the base of the old tree stump. From somewhere deep in the mists, sounded a peal of chapel bells.

The lake, tranquil as ever, slipped seamlessly into the magic of dream-time. The garden was at peace, with its secrets.

And still the dormouse slept.

POEMS

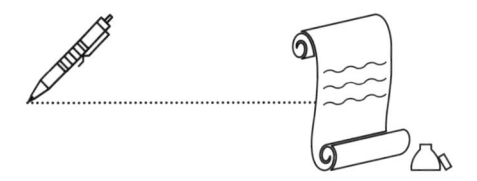

PEREGRINES ON THE CLOCK TOWER

These poems were inspired by 'The Peregrine Diaries' on page 30

THE TIERCEL

Perched on a stone cherub
above a boneyard of birds
with his brutal beak, hangman's hood,
he was hardly angelic;
only the white eye-lid flickering,
this moist, nictitating membrane
briefly blotting out the black eye.

Then hooked on the sky,
arcing for the stoop,
with fierce, ebony talons,
and eerie, piercing cry.

'KEK-KEK! KEK-KEK!'

THE FALCON

Yet, watching a chick through a scope,
the female falcon,
flapping and hopping on bone ledge,
playing with the carcass of a pigeon
as a kitten, or puppy, would play with a toy –
was almost comical.

Yet she soon would stoop from the sun,
with an adult's precision,
a perfect, peregrine incision –
slicing the sky.

N.B. A tiercel is the name given to a male peregrine falcon. Tiercel is French for 'third' and the male peregrine is a third smaller than the female, which is called a falcon.

SEA LAMPREY

This poem was inspired by the article 'Sea Lamprey', on page 37

Watching sea lamprey spawn,
in an outlet of the Taff,
the male
shifting huge stones
so carefully,
with his oval, suckered mouth;
creating a redd,
a dowry for his mate,
was quite a rare sight.

And as their love-making continued
and their mottled backs entwined,
I found it hard to fathom
how that same, attentive mouth,
with its bony, razor-like tongue
could bore into victims;
secreted saliva
preventing blood from clotting,
as the vampire's teeth
rasped onto flesh,
sucking the life
out of a salmon or sea trout.

In days,
both lamprey would be dead,
devoured by eels;
returned to the void.

SHOALING

Leaves litter a rippling surface,
broken by the plop of a float
and casting deep for frenzied fish
men sight their poles with telescopic eyes,
then float in weeds which choke the bank
hooked by bait which they must thank
for keeping full the nets that drift,
with the current, full of fish.

Gudgeon, goldfish, minnows, roach,
victims of the catapult,
hungry for the maggots' drop
eager for the deadly plop.
And so in shoals men watch their poles
on stalks which trawl the limpid light,
hid amongst the knot of weeds,
hooked by bait which fish might bite.

This poem was previously published in *The Countryman* magazine.

THE GHOSTS OF GREENFARM HOSTEL

I used to work nights in a homeless hostel on the outskirts of Cardiff. It was an isolated place, very rural in character, with huge gardens close to a large cemetery. Greenfarm Hostel had been the site of human habitation for many centuries, and there was evidence of Roman settlements in the area. The gardens contained a number of very large trees, and I knew tawny owls were nesting in one of these. And although I had never seen an owl, I had heard their haunting cries from time to time.

On one particular moonlit night, with the mists rolling in from the direction of the cemetery, I happened to open the back door to get a breath of fresh air, only to glimpse the fleeting form of a tawny owl vanish into the blackness. Its eerie cry sent an icy chill down my spine. I was inspired to write the poem on the next page about my experience.

OWL NIGHT

I imagined them coupling
outside in the storm
in ivy-clad oak,
all beaks and claws
and a flurry of feathers.

And the dowry,
a fat rat –
guts glistening in the moonlight.

And foraging for food,
ears pricked for the slightest sound,
bright eyes mounted on chiselled cheekbones,
a pretty dormouse
shivers at the margins of mist.

In pellets
the shattered bones
of shrews and mice.

This poem was previously published in *The Countryman* magazine.

CONGER

Man's waist thick,
fathomed at depth,
wrecking jaws,
wrecking flesh.

Spawned in black,
greased against the sea;
hooked and trawled,
gaffed, clubbed,
and clubbed again on the neck.

Then pictured on paper,
malevolent in death;
longer than a man's body.

THE RIVER BECKONS FOR A LAST CAST

I wink at you through splinters of starlight,
weeds trail like green limbs
and as coracles swirl in your subconscious,
I know I'll pull you in.

So bury me in a creel made of wicker
and make this my last cast,
drop me in a favourite river,
but do not stand on the bank and weep.

Think of the time we cast a line
on Twyi, Teifi, Taff,
and dream in the reeds where the bittern cries
and swallows sweep flies from the shallows.

And where the river narrows,
where the big trout lie,
think fondly of old Dai;
of recollections
swan-white reflections
and foxgloves fingered by bees,
and when the wind breathes
before storm clouds intercede,
maybe, just maybe, I'll sense your soft shoe shuffle.

So bury me in a creel made of wicker
and make this my last cast,
but do not stand on the bank and weep;
I am not dead, but in your sleep.

This poem was previously published in *Agenda, The Magazine of the Wild Trout Trust*, and *Fallon's Angler*.

THE WYE

In the slack current
beneath the surface tension
where sewin slip through weeds like glass,
the deep dreams.

Of creep of the otter,
sleep of the silver eel,
moon-filled pools
first run of sea-lice salmon.

Coracles swirl,
rush of nymphs to the interface,
air and water,
siblings of the sun.

This poem was previously published in *Fallon's Angler*.

SPATE

Brown and turgid the river ran,
netting cans, bottles and floating footballs.
The footfalls of otters
and stink of mink are washed away,
the kingfisher's latrine too.

Below the weir,
which steams with spray,
salmon and peal seek solace in holes,
scent the gravel redds,
the mingling
of milt and eggs.

Now,
sentient, like all around,
the river roars
and swallows sound.

THE RIVER'S MIDDEN

The river's midden
is its banks and trees.

After the deluge,
what once remained hidden,
now litters those banks
and leaves those trees.

I once found an eel,
Three pounds, at least,
crow-pecked
and curled like a swirl of liquorice,
hanging from the branches
of a weeping willow.

Eels, at the best of times,
rarely ever please.

THE FISH MARKET

Glass-eyed fish glare,
unwrapped on their pall of ice;
from what depths were you trawled
cod, hake, lemon sole?

Sea-scent fuses with air,
eyes stare,
at young wives, old men.
And do you like them staring
when, ghosts haunt another place
reverent of your living race?

And when in death we pay no heed,
for with sharp knives we make you bleed,
then will your ghosts return to taunt
ink-black waters that our trawlers haunt.

RIVER DREAMS

Spun
in a weed-strewn moon's reflection,
are recollections
where coracles swirled in salmon pools
on Twyi, Teifi, Taff,
of Dai the ferryman,
rock for a pillow,
sound asleep.

Where otters creep,
willows weep shade into water canvas;
brush of feather-blue,
crush of lover's limbs,
cool summer pools.

In the dew,
spirit's feet,
where two tides meet,
and 'Croeso I Gymru',
becomes 'Welcome to Wales'.

This poem was previously published in *Agenda*, and *Fallon's Angler*.

VIEW FROM A RIVER BRIDGE

And the night's trains
clattering to the station,
their glow-worm lights,
and swan-white reflections;
then recollections of a reflected light,
of a night when pink skies
swam on a rippling surface,
and tangerine lamplights
flickered amongst those clouds,
like setting suns.

This poem was previously published in *The Countryman* magazine.

A RIVER SENSES A JOGGER AT NIGHT

In secret,
I admire your smoothness,
lycra-clad limbs.

I wink at you through splinters of starlight.
On the bridge,
sense your soft shoe shuffle,
bounce of your breasts.

Weeds trail like green limbs,
I long to caress,
pull you in,
lay your head on my pillow pebbles,
kiss you,
with my liquid lips.

Lie on my water bed.